Alice & Daisy

EDWARDIAN RAG DOLL SISTERS
TO MAKE AND DRESS

Valerie Janitch

Photography by
Gary Sinfield

Nexus Special Interests

Nexus Special Interests Ltd.
Nexus House
Azalea Drive
Swanley
Kent BR8 8HU

First published by Nexus Special Interests Ltd., 1998

ISBN 1-85486-183-2

Typeset by Kate Williams, Abergavenny.
Printed and bound in Great Britain by Biddles Ltd., Guildford & King's Lynn.

Alice & Daisy

Contents

Acknowledgements

I would like to thank the following:

Beverly Laughlin for all her enthusiastic encouragement and support.

Lyn Corson for being the ideal editor – extremely efficient but author-friendly too!

Kate Williams for making my boring manuscript look so attractive.

Helen Dunbar for her advice and help with the props and decorations for the sisters' home.

Chris Kingdom and **Rosemary Pinkney** for all the beautiful *Offray* ribbons that trim Alice and Daisy's clothes and their furniture.

UHU for both *UHU All-Purpose Clear Adhesive*, *UHU Action* + fabric glue and *UHU Stic* paper glue.

Gary Sinfield for his imaginative photography – and his patience!

Introduction, guidelines and helpful hints

Introduction

The two rag dolls, Alice and Daisy, are in love with fashion – and with their slender hourglass figures, is it surprising! They look elegant and pretty, whatever they wear: so they spend a lot of time dressing up and admiring themselves in the mirror. From warm winter cloaks and bonnets down to lace-trimmed petticoats and pantalettes, all their outfits are so flattering that it's hard to decide which to choose. Of course, Alice and Daisy would be happiest if you made them all!

Guidelines and helpful hints

Here are some useful tips to bear in mind as you make and dress your doll. They will help to make the job as easy as possible, and ensure a really professional result.

The fabrics to use

The dolls themselves are made from medium-weight cream cotton poplin from the dress fabric department, and their clothes are small amounts of lingerie lawn or cotton-type dress fabric or felt. Cotton-type fabrics are best for most things – look for a firm, close weave, and avoid silky man-made fabrics which usually fray. But if you can't avoid using a fabric with a tendency to fray, treat the cut edge with a special fray check product, or *UHU Action+* fabric glue, both of which are available from haberdashery departments.

If you have difficulty finding anything sufficiently dainty for the undies, you might find a suitable voile in the curtain net department. Summer dress fabrics are generally the ideal weight for most other things, but sometimes plain or printed cotton sheeting can be very effective, as you can see in Alice's pink skirt (Chapter 3). However, don't try to use thick woven fabrics which are too bulky for such small garments – felt is usually a good alternative.

When you *are* using felt, make sure you buy a good quality which is firm and an even thickness. Thin, poorly made felt is a waste of time, because the seams will pull apart.

Stuffing

Although it must never be seen, this is the most important part of the doll! Use the best quality soft toy stuffing (make sure it is certified pure and flameproof). When you come to stuff your doll, read all the notes in **Chapter 1 Making the basic rag doll**, and follow them very carefully. Remember to stitch extra strong seams, so that they don't burst open when you stuff!

Wool for the hair

I like to use embroidery wool for the hair, because the range of colours available offers such a good choice of realistic hair shades – these are not generally so easy to find in knitting yarns – however, knitting yarn does the job just as well. Simply cut it into 76 cm (30 in) lengths, remembering that the thicker the yarn, the fewer pieces you will need (the embroidery wool recommended here is only two-ply, but the finest knitting yarns are usually three- or four-ply, and many are even thicker).

Making your patterns

Trace the patterns onto ordinary household greaseproof paper, taking care to fold the paper *when this is stipulated* (when only the word FOLD is shown it indicates a fold in the fabric). Trace all the markings including arrows, and note the name of the piece and which part of the garment it is, also when it has to be reversed to cut a second piece. If you have traced the pattern onto folded paper, trace all the markings through to the other side before opening it up.

You will find that when there is a large pattern piece that is a simple shape, such as a skirt, it is shown as a diagram indicating the measurements for you to make your own pattern. The easiest way to do this is to use a large sheet of graph paper (or special pattern drawing squared paper available in haberdashery departments). Place this flat on the table with a sheet of tracing paper on top. Then simply use a ruler to draw out the specified measurements, following the printed lines of the squared paper underneath. It is a wise precaution to fix the sheets together with paperclips or tape while you measure. *Note*: you will find a sheet of graph paper printed at the back of the book. This can be photocopied twice or four times, and then carefully taped together, to make a large background sheet.

Following the directions

The instructions are numbered step by step, and it is always a good idea to read through the *whole* of each step, even though it may contain several operations. This will give you a clear picture of what you are aiming to achieve at each stage and make it easier to understand each part of it.

Cutting out

Pin the pattern pieces to the wrong side of the fabric, noting carefully when a fold is indicated. The arrows show the straight of the fabric (the 'up and down' of the weave) – the arrow should be parallel to the selvedge when the pattern is placed on the fabric. There are no arrows on pieces to be cut in felt – as felt is not woven it can be cut in any direction.

When a piece is marked REVERSE, this means that it must be turned over to cut the second piece. If you cut the shape in folded fabric (right side inside), you can cut both pieces at the same time and the pattern will be automatically reversed for the second piece.

Cut out carefully, using fairly small, pointed scissors for the detailed pieces. Then transfer all the notches and dots to each piece of fabric, using a chalk pencil or disappearing marker.

Seams

Approximately 5 mm (¼ in) is allowed for seams on fabric, and approximately 3 mm (⅛ in) for felt, which should be oversewn to join (see below).

Always work with right sides together, unless otherwise stated. Pin the pieces together before stitching each seam, matching any markings very carefully. Ordinary 2.5 cm (1 in) dressmakers' pins are generally very satisfactory, but if you are working on a particularly delicate fabric, 'lace' or 'wedding dress' pins are specially fine, and won't leave a mark.

Sewing

You can sew either by hand or machine, although short seams, setting-in sleeves, etc. are often quicker and neater when done by hand. Also, felt seams should be oversewn with small stitches, quite close together, and I find it makes a softer join when this is done by hand.

Use regular sewing thread, but it is a good idea to use it double for the doll itself, and also when making a long line of gathers, as for a skirt.

Before turning to the right side, clip curves and corners neatly. This is really important in order to achieve a professional finish on such tiny garments.

Press all seams open. It is not always practical to use an iron on this small scale so when this happens, use your thumbnail.

Making neat hems

When using a lightweight fabric, it is usually possible to turn under a double hem and still retain a natural look. But for the medium-weight fabrics which are most often used in these designs, it is less bulky and therefore more attractive to turn hems under only once and herringbone-stitch over the raw edge (see diagram).

When doing this try, if possible, to cut the fabric straight along a thread. This will give a neater finish on the wrong side, as well as preventing unnecessary fraying.

Elastic

Narrow round elastic (not shirring elastic) is ideal. When using it to draw up wrists etc., you can, if you prefer, herringbone-stitch the elastic into position with double thread over the top, then draw it up as required and either stitch the cut ends, or make a secure knot. This avoids threading it through a channel.

Snap fasteners

This is usually the best way to fasten the garments. The most suitable ones to use on this scale are 7 mm (¼ in) and transparent. These are thin enough to avoid any bulkiness, and are almost invisible in use. They are also flexible, which makes them easy to sew on as well as to open and close.

Trimmings to choose

Trimmings are plentiful and pretty – lots of lace and broderie anglaise with touches of braid and flowers (both of which you can make yourself, if you wish). In fact, just the sort of thing any turn-of-the-century young lady of fashion *would* select to trim her clothes.

Don't choose the finest lace edgings – you will find something a little sturdier is more effective – look for the daintiest broderie anglaise (eyelet embroidery) you can find, and search for ribbons that either tone or contrast well with your fabric so that they really complement the garment. All the ribbons used in this book are by *Offray*, who have a wonderful range of shades, especially in single-face, which are usually the most suitable.

Glue

Trimmings are usually most easily and satisfactorily fixed with glue. Use a clear all-purpose adhesive like *UHU*, which is quick-drying and gives a very firm hold.

Measurements

Use either metric or imperial measurements, but *don't* compare the two because they may not be the same. Each design has been worked out individually to make it as simple as possible and avoid the eye-strain of counting tiny measurements!

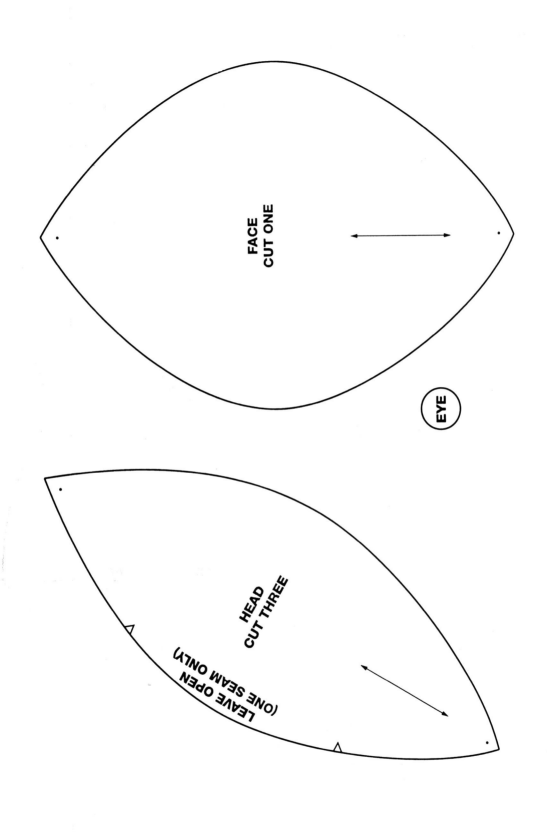

FACE
CUT ONE

EYE

HEAD
CUT THREE

LEAVE OPEN
(ONE SEAM ONLY)

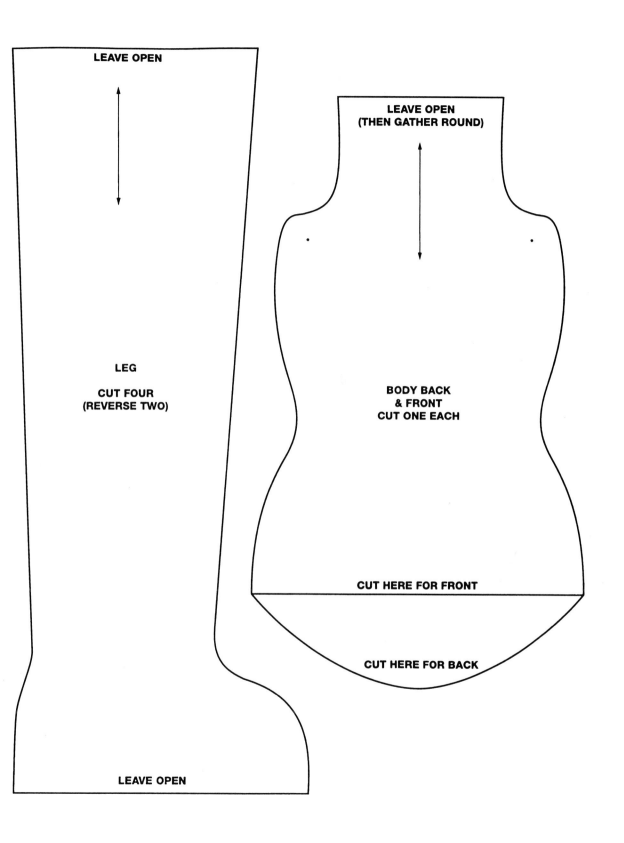

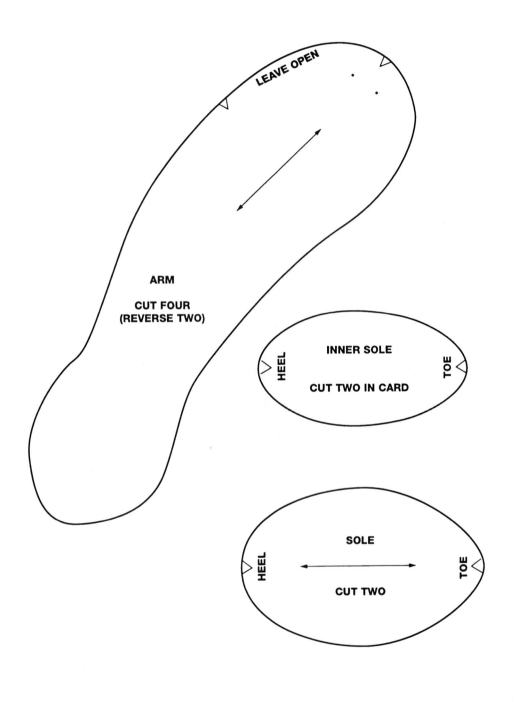

LEAVE OPEN

ARM

CUT FOUR
(REVERSE TWO)

INNER SOLE

HEEL

TOE

CUT TWO IN CARD

SOLE

HEEL

TOE

CUT TWO

Chapter 1
Making the basic rag doll

Remember, the secret of a happy rag doll lies in the stuffing! It has to be smooth and *very* firm. Push tiny pieces of filling into small areas like hands and feet, building the stuffing up slowly so that the surface is smooth on the outside. Always tease the stuffing out before inserting it, to avoid lumpiness. Use larger pieces as you reach wider areas, but still make sure the filling is pushed well into all the corners and curves.

When the stuffing is completed and the seams closed, roll each piece between your hands to achieve a really smooth finish. This applies particularly to the head, which should be rolled between the palms to make it a smoothly rounded, very firm ball. As already emphasised, the whole doll should be very firmly stuffed, to ensure that it keeps its shape and doesn't become limp with loving! However, the head should be very, *very* tightly stuffed – my rule is to stuff it until it seems you can't get any more filling in ... and then add some more! Close the seam with double thread: if you have to pull the edges tightly across the bulging filling, you'll know you've done a good job! (Don't worry if your closing seam isn't very neat as it will be hidden by the hair.)

You will need (for each doll):

- 30 cm (12 in) cream medium-weight cotton poplin, 90 cm (36 in) wide
- Polyester stuffing
- 2 skeins of *Twilleys* stranded embroidery wool for the hair (Alice's hair is shade 1184 and Daisy's is shade 1113), or use knitting yarn
- 2 cm × 4 cm (¾ in × 1½ in) dark brown felt, for the eyes
- 2 small black domed sequins, for the pupils
- Pinky-red stranded embroidery cotton, for the mouth (sewing thread will do)
- Matching and black sewing threads
- Stiff card, for inner soles (or use a margarine, yogurt or similar carton lid if a washable stiffening is required)
- Clear adhesive (*UHU* all-purpose adhesive is recommended)
- A strong darning needle
- Pinking shears (optional)

1 Cut the back once, following the pattern: then cut the pattern again for the front, but this time cut straight across the lower edge, as indicated. Cut the arm and leg twice each in *double* fabric. Cut the face once, the head three times and the sole twice. Cut the inner sole twice in card (or alternative).

2 Mark notches at the top of the arms, on *one* head piece, and on the soles. Mark dots on the face and head pieces.

3 To make each leg, join two pieces along the front and back seams, leaving the upper and lower edges open. Clip the curves (see Fig 1: clipping diagram).

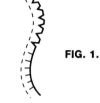

FIG. 1.

CLIPPING OUTWARD AND INWARD CURVES

There are two ways to make the feet. The first is more realistically rounded, but the second is a little easier. Neither shows when the doll is wearing shoes, so it doesn't really matter which you choose.

Version (a) Fit the sole inside the lower edge, matching notches to seams, and stitch neatly into position. Trim the seam and turn to the right side. Fit the stiff inner sole inside, holding it temporarily in position with pins from the outside (Fig 2).

FIG. 2.

Version (b) Turn the leg to the right side. Turn the lower edge under and tack. Place the stiff inner sole on top of the fabric sole, matching notches (Fig 3a). Run a trail of glue all round close to the outer edge of the fabric: bring the fabric smoothly over the edge of the card and press it down on top (Fig 3b). Pin the sole to the bottom of the foot, wrong side inside, matching notches to front and back seams, then oversew the edges neatly together all round (Fig 3c).

FIG. 3a.

INNER SOLE

FIG. 3b.

Stuff the foot and leg firmly to the top of the leg (see stuffing notes at the beginning of this chapter). Then place the *front and back seams together*, raw edges level, and gather across the top, drawing up to measure 3 cm (1¼ in). Fasten off securely.

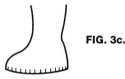

FIG. 3c.

4 Join the side seams of the body, leaving the neck and lower edges open. Turn up the lower edge and tack. Clip the curves (Fig 1) and turn to the right side. Stuff firmly, pushing the filling well up into the shoulders. When nearly stuffed, mark the lower edge centres back and front, then pin the top of one leg inside the *front*

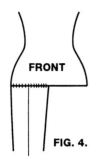

FIG. 4.

BODY

FIG. 5.

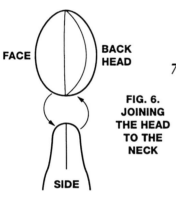

FACE
BACK HEAD
SIDE

FIG. 6.
JOINING
THE HEAD
TO THE
NECK

FIG. 7.
LADDER STITCH

lower edge, between the side and centre, and stitch it neatly into place (Fig 4). Repeat with the other leg. Stitch the lower edge of the back across the back of *one* leg only, easing it in to fit (the back edge of the body will ease naturally into the leg gathers). Now push more filling into the waist and hips, so that the lower body is firmly stuffed. Then stitch across the back of the second leg in the same way.

5 Stuff the neck, pushing the filling well down into the shoulders. When firmly stuffed almost to the top, gather the raw edge and draw it up, stitch *across* the gathers, to make it as flat as possible on top (Fig 5).

6 Stitch a head piece to each side of the face, matching the dots carefully. Stitch the third head piece between the other two, leaving one seam open between the notches. Turn the raw edges to the inside and tack. Trim and clip the seams (using pinking shears if possible) and turn to the right side. Stuff very firmly indeed (see beginning of chapter), then close the seam and mould into shape as directed.

7 Using double thread, take a stitch through the base of the head from back to front, then take another through the top of the neck, from front to back (Fig 6). Repeat the first stitch and draw up, so that the head is held in position. Take another stitch through the neck, then repeat from side to side to position the head even more accurately, and finish off.

Still using double thread, ladder-stitch the head and neck together all round, taking small stitches alternately through the head and neck and pulling tight between each (Fig 7). Go round twice in this way.

8 To make each arm, stitch two pieces together all round, leaving open between the notches. Turn the raw edges to the inside and tack. Clip the seam (especially carefully round the wrist and hand), then turn to the right side and stuff firmly before slip-stitching the edges of the seam neatly together.

9 Using double thread, stitch the arms to the body, taking alternate stitches through the dots marked on the arm and shoulder. Stitch very firmly and finish off securely.

Alice and Daisy's hairstyles

1 First separate the strands of embroidery wool and then place them together again, making sure all the cut ends are exactly level at each end. (It is *essential to* separate the strands of embroidery wool in this way, in order to make a full head of realistic-looking hair.) If using knitting yarn, cut it into 76 cm (30 in) lengths, remembering that the thicker the yarn, the fewer strands you will need compared to the embroidery wool, which is only two-ply (there are 72 strands in each skein).

2 **Alice:** Reserve half a skein (36 strands) for her topknot. Remove three more strands to sew with.

3 Fold the remaining hank in half, cut ends exactly together, and cut across the fold keeping all the strands together.

4 Mark the seam at each side of the face with a pin, 2 cm (¾ in) above the head/neck join (Fig 8).

FIG. 8.

5 Thread a strong darning needle with a single strand of wool and knot the end, then push it through the centre back of the head, 3 cm (1¼ in) behind the centre top join. Bring it out again at the centre front, 2.5 cm (1 in) below the centre top (see dot on Fig 8). Place the strands of wool across the top of the head between these two points, then take the single strand back over them and make a small stitch over the knot, pulling the wool tight to hold the strands in place. Take the strand back over the top and push the needle through again, this time from front to back. Pull tight and finish off securely.

6 Spread the strands out smoothly over the head, then count fifty strands at each side of the face and stitch them directly behind the seam at the point marked with a pin.

7 Lift up the section of hair behind one of these side pieces and spread glue over the fabric underneath, then press

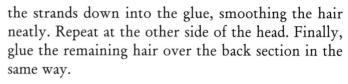

the strands down into the glue, smoothing the hair neatly. Repeat at the other side of the head. Finally, glue the remaining hair over the back section in the same way.

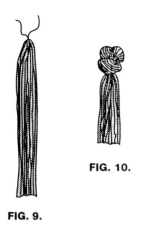

FIG. 10.

FIG. 9.

8 For her topknot, tie the reserved strands at the centre with a single 25 cm (10 in) long strand and fold in half at this point (Fig 9). Knot the resulting hank loosely at the folded top end, approximately 16 cm (6½ in) above the cut ends. Tuck the tied top down behind the knot, then bring the ends of the single strand round the hank and tie them quite loosely underneath the knotted strands (Fig 10). Stitch to the crown of the head, the cut ends hanging down behind.

9 Trim the cut ends neatly to length all round.

10 **Daisy:** Use half a skein (36 strands) for her fringe. Remove three more strands to sew with.

FIG. 11.

11 Tie the fringe strands at the centre with a coloured thread, then fold them in half at this point. Mark both the side head panels centrally with a pin, 1.5 cm (⅝ in) below the centre top join (Fig 11).

Thread a strong darning needle with a single strand of wool and knot the end, then push it through one of the marked points and bring it out at the other one. Place the fringe strands over the top of the head, the tied centre level with the *middle* of the face (Fig 11), and the cut ends hanging down at the back. Take the single strand back over the fringe strands and then stitch across them so that they are held securely in place.

12 Working over the top of the fringe strands, follow the directions for Alice from Step 3 to Step 7 inclusive.

13 Remove the coloured thread and cut the strands across the fold, then trim the fringe to shape.

14 Trim the cut ends neatly to length all round.

The finishing touch – faces and features

Once you have done the hairstyle, you have already begun to create your own doll's individual character. You can see from the photographs how their hairstyles help to suggest that Alice is a rather demure little girl, whilst Daisy has a slightly mischievous nature. Alice is the quiet, practical one – Daisy is a bit adventurous! However, it is the facial features that complete the whole story. The expression says it all: sweet or sour, happy or sad, merry or melancholy, serene or thoughtful.

Unless you are an expert with your needle and are anxious to create an exquisite piece of detailed embroidery, follow my example, and keep it simple. You can see from the colour photographs that my dolls have round felt eyes with sequin centres, sewn on with straight stitches. More straight stitches make the eyebrows and pert little nose, and the cute smile is just a curve of stem stitch. So if you are one of the many potential dollmakers put off by the prospect of having to create an attractive face, don't be – when it's as simple as this, you really can't go wrong! If you're not satisfied with one or other element, just take it out and start over again.

1 Begin with the eyes, cutting them in dark brown felt. Use black if you like, but I prefer the softer effect of dark brown contrasted with a black sequin. If, on the other hand, you would prefer blue or green eyes, be careful – you need the density of a fairly dark shade to get the right effect, so choose a dark azure blue, a strong grey-blue or a deep olive green.

    You might like to share my special way of cutting a really accurate small circle as I used to find it very difficult to cut round the tiny pattern. Find a round object with a sharp edge that is the same size as the pattern (I use the cap of a ballpoint pen: for larger circles, it could be a thimble or the plastic cap of a chemist's pill container). You will also need either a piece of light-coloured chalk, a wax crayon or coloured pencil (talcum powder will do if you haven't anything else). Rub this quite generously over the rim of the round object, then press it down firmly on the felt, twisting it round without moving the position as if using a pastry cutter to make jam tarts. This will leave a clear line round which to cut with sharp scissors. Use this for the back of the eye, just in case there are any marks left on it.

2 In order to determine the position of the eyes on the face, put each sequin on a pin and then push it through a felt eye (dome side up). Move them around until you are satisfied. The first time you do this, you may find that you have placed the eyes much too high up, so it's worth moving them down quite a bit, even as far as half-way down the face, to see if they look better there – you might be quite surprised! (Have a look at Alice and Daisy if you need guidance.)

FACE:

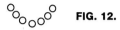
FIG. 12.

FIG. 13.

FIG. 14.

3 When you are happy with the eyes, mark the position of the nose with a pin. It should be level with the lower edge of the eyes and exactly central.

4 Now mark the mouth, again with pins. Begin at the centre, about 1 cm (⅜ in) below the nose, building it up with pairs of pins, one at each side, until you have just the expression you want (Fig 12). If you want a happy smile, like Alice and Daisy, make the pins curve up so that the mouth is just a fraction *more* 'smiley' than you wish it to be. If you would prefer something a little more coy, try making a 'U' shape instead of the regular curve described above.

5 Check that you are absolutely satisfied with the doll's expression. If not, rearrange the components until you are (Fig 13).

6 Stitch the eyes into place with black thread (use it double if the effect is not strong enough), making eight straight stitches from the centre of the sequin to just a little *beyond* the edge of the felt (Fig 14).

7 Make a very tiny straight stitch, again with black thread, for the nose.

8 Use two strands of embroidery (or sewing) cotton for the mouth. Push the needle through from the side of the head, just behind the seam (drawing back the hair). Remove the first pin at one side and bring the needle through the hole that remains. Remove the next pin and make the first stitch through that hole, bringing the needle out again through the first hole. Then continue to stem-stitch round the mouth in this way, finishing off at the other side of the head.

When dressing your doll, you will find it much easier to fit dresses, skirts, petticoats etc. from the feet up – rather than over the head and down! Also you may prefer to slip the petticoat on last, to prevent it being crushed as you put the garment on over it.

Chapter 2

Petticoats, pantalettes and camisoles

Dainty underpinnings are an essential for any well-dressed rag doll. Use a lightweight fabric, so that it won't be bulky under her top garments. Alice chose a very finely striped cotton and matching embroidered lace. Daisy decided on snowy white, sprigged with palest blue flowers – romantically trimmed with rows of crisp white lace and tiny blue bows.

You will need:

- 30 cm (12 in) lightweight cotton-type fabric, 90 cm (36 in) wide (for each doll)
- 1.2 m (1⅜ yd) double-edged lace, 2 cm (¾ in) wide (Alice)
- 2.8 m (3¼ yd) lace, 1 cm (⅜ in) deep (Daisy)
- 60 cm (¾ yd) single-face satin ribbon, 5 mm (¼ in) wide – for bows (Daisy)
- 20 cm (¼ yd) feather-edge satin ribbon, 5 mm (¼ in) wide – for shoulder straps (Daisy)
- 60 cm (24 in) narrow round elastic (for each doll)
- 2 snap fasteners (for each doll)
- Matching sewing threads

1 Cut a piece of fabric for the petticoat 20 cm × 55 cm (8 in × 21½ in) as Fig 1. Cut the camisole pattern once and the pantalettes twice.

2 Join the inner leg seam of each pantalettes piece between A–B. Then, right sides together, join the two pieces between C–A–C (Fig 2). Clip the curve carefully.

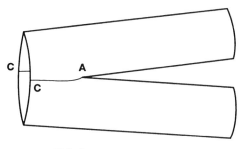

FIG. 2.

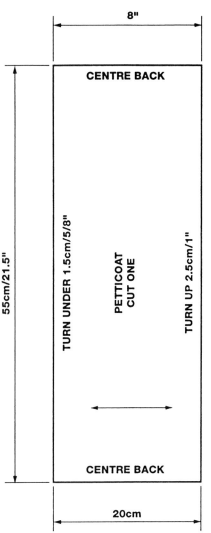

FIG. 1.

3 Fold the top edge over, turning the raw edge under as indicated, and hem.

4 Turn up the bottom of each leg, as indicated. Turn the raw edge under, and hem. Then stitch again, 1 cm (⅜ in) below, to form a channel for the elastic (Fig 3).

5 Turn to the right side and, for Alice, stitch lace 1 cm (⅜ in) above the lower edge of each leg (Fig 4). For Daisy, stitch one row of lace

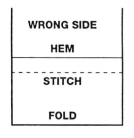

FIG. 3

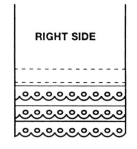

FIG. 3

FIG. 3

19

slightly overlapping the lower edge: another row directly below the lower stitching line of the elastic channel, and a final row between the first two (Fig 5).

6 Thread elastic through waist and leg hems, draw up to fit and knot securely.

7 Join the side edges of the petticoat to form the centre back seam.

8 Turn the top edge over and make a hem as for the pantalettes (Step 3).

9 Turn up a 2.5 cm (1 in) hem, turning the raw edge under, and stitch.

10 Turn to the right side and trim Alice's hem with lace, 1 cm (⅜ in) above the edge. Stitch three rows of lace round Daisy's hem to match her pantalettes.

11 Thread elastic through the waist and draw up to fit.

12 Turn under the centre back edges of the camisole and herringbone-stitch over the raw edge. Make 5 mm (¼ in) hems along the top and bottom edges in the same way.

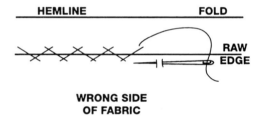

HEMLINE   **FOLD**

RAW EDGE

WRONG SIDE OF FABRIC

DIAGRAM SHOWING HERRINGBONE STITCH

13 Stitch lace along the top, very slightly overlapping the edge.

14 Sew snap fasteners at the top and centre of the back opening, as indicated.

15 Fit the camisole on the doll and pin 8 cm (3¼ in) lengths of lace (for Alice) or ribbon (for Daisy) in position for the shoulder straps. Remove the camisole and stitch the straps inside at the back and front *1.5 cm (⅝ in) below the top edge,* to allow easy access for arms.

16 Finally, make butterfly bows to trim Daisy's undies (see Trims: Chapter 10). Use 7 cm (2¾ in) lengths of ribbon, and measure points B and C 4 cm (⅝ in) apart. Stitch two bows to the camisole, one over the front stitching line of each strap. Stitch one bow to each leg of the pantalettes, directly opposite the inner leg seam and just below the elastic, and stitch four down the centre front of the petticoat, as illustrated, spacing them 3 cm (1¼ in) apart.

17 To dress either doll, put the camisole on first, followed by the petticoat. Put the pantalettes on last, tucking the lower edge of the camisole neatly inside them.

Instructions for Alice and Daisy's **shoes** are in Chapter 9 (Accessories).

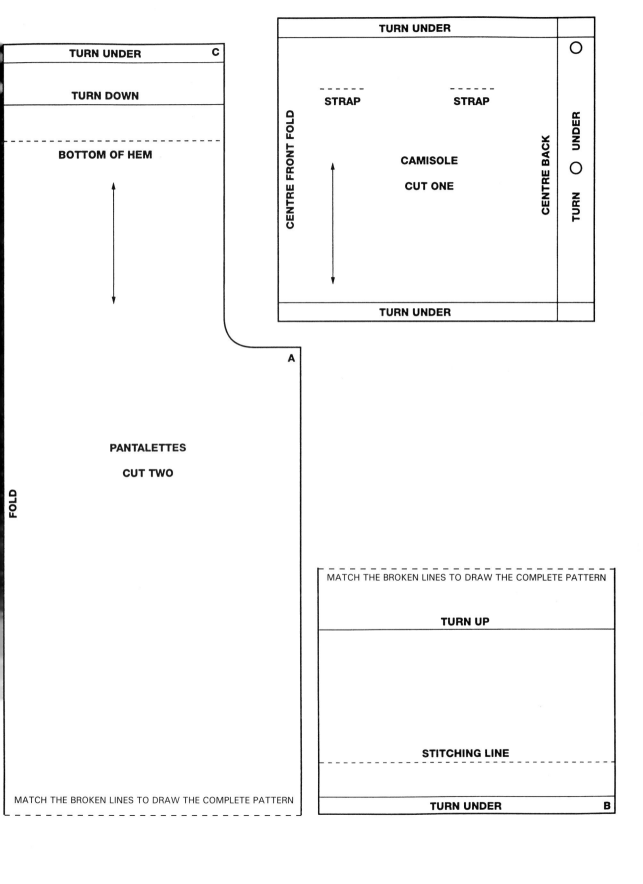

TURN UNDER   **C**

TURN DOWN

BOTTOM OF HEM

CENTRE FRONT FOLD

TURN UNDER

STRAP   **STRAP**

CAMISOLE

CUT ONE

CENTRE BACK

TURN UNDER

TURN UNDER

PANTALETTES

CUT TWO

FOLD

MATCH THE BROKEN LINES TO DRAW THE COMPLETE PATTERN

MATCH THE BROKEN LINES TO DRAW THE COMPLETE PATTERN

TURN UP

STITCHING LINE

TURN UNDER   **B**

A fine cotton lawn is the ideal fabric to use for dainty undies, because it is thin enough not to create any bulkiness that might spoil the effect of the garments on top, but don't choose silky man-made fabrics, even if they look suitable, because they will probably fray and cause you all kinds of problems. Lawn is lovely to work with, especially if you are sewing by hand, because the needle slides through so easily – and seams are pressed open with one's thumbnail. Cotton lawn is generally very inexpensive, and you can often find it even cheaper in markets. Avoid big, bold prints: if you can't find a really small, dainty design, a plain fabric is much safer, either in white or a soft pastel colour, then you can go overboard with the trimmings – which are far more important anyway. Finding suitable lace, ribbons and embroidered motifs is usually much easier.

You won't be short of inspiration if your needlecraft shop or department store has a good stock of trimmings, and if the selection is so good that you find choosing difficult, take your dolls along and let them help. It is often very useful to have the doll with you, as you will gain a far better sense of scale and proportion if you can actually see a fabric or trimming against the doll who is going to wear it, and the garment it is going to trim.

Your dolls will probably choose the most expensive lace edgings and broderie anglaise in sight, and demand extravagant double satin ribbons. Although lace and broderie anglaise are the essential 'icing on the cake' for pretty underpinnings, they can be very expensive, but you will usually be able to find something cheaper. The vital thing to remember is to keep everything small – the design itself, the repeat pattern and the depth. Be careful with broderie anglaise, which can look so pretty in the shop, but surprisingly out of proportion when you apply it to the garment it is intended to trim.

In most cases, it is far more effective to have two or three rows of narrow trimming rather than one row of a deeper one, which may look too heavy. Look for the cheapest narrow lace, 5 mm (¼ in) and 1 cm (⅜ in) deep and buy plenty of it. Lace often looks even prettier when it is gathered, so if you want frills and flounces where flat lace is shown, buy half as much again as the amount stated in the list of materials, then gather the straight edge before you apply it and don't draw up the gathers until you have pinned the lace evenly into position.

There are lots of temptations if you want ideas for romantic finishing touches for your dolls' luxury lingerie. Machine-embroidered flowers or tiny guipure lace daisies or hearts (both by the metre or yard) are perfect, and you will need only a short length if you cut the motifs up and use them individually. You can also buy ready-made ribbon roses and tiny bows, if you can't be bothered to make your own.

As for ribbons, the same rule applies: the wider the ribbon, the heavier and more out of proportion it will look. Narrow ribbons made into tiny butterfly bows are enchanting – and again you won't need to buy very much – 1.5 mm (1/16 in), 3 mm (⅛ in) and 5–7 mm (¼ in) are the widths to look for. In the latter widths, single-face ribbon is daintier and easier to work with than the more expensive double-face satin.

Chapter 3

Blouses and skirts
– romantic and nautical

Blouses and skirts play contrasting roles in the sisters' wardrobe. They can be frilly and feminine, like Alice's pink flowered top and matching deep rose skirt – or fresh as a sea breeze, like Daisy's jaunty sailor outfit. I used a lightweight printed cotton to emphasise the soft lines of Alice's blouse, whilst Daisy's crisp white version is an only slightly more substantial medium-weight poplin. Any medium-weight cotton-type fabric would do for the skirts, though I have used cotton sheeting for these. This is a useful fabric if you want a fabric with little more substance – but beware using it for dresses, unless you want a rather stiff or starched effect.

You will need:

- ✂ 18 cm × 70 cm (7 in × 28 in) light to medium weight cotton-type fabric, for the blouse
- ✂ 20 cm (¼ yd) medium-weight cotton-type fabric, 90 cm (36 in) wide, for Alice's skirt, or Daisy's skirt and collar
- ✂ 60 cm (⅝ yd) lace, 2 cm (¾ in) deep, for Alice's blouse
- ✂ 12 cm (5 in) matching bias binding, for the neck of either blouse
- ✂ 45 cm (½ yd) white bias binding, for Daisy's collar
- ✂ 11 cm (4½ in) red satin ribbon, 9 mm (⅜ in) wide, for Daisy's collar
- ✂ 60 cm (¾ yd) white satin ribbon, 1.5 mm (¹⁄₁₆ in) wide, for Daisy's skirt
- ✂ 35 cm (½ yd) very narrow matching braid, for Alice's waistband
- ✂ 3 cm × 15 cm (1¼ × 6 in) heavy Vilene, for Alice's waistband
- ✂ 20 cm (8 in) narrow round elastic, for either blouse
- ✂ 3 snap fasteners for the blouse, one for the skirt, and two for Daisy's collar
- ✂ Matching sewing threads
- ✂ Clear adhesive to fix the braid on Alice's waistband

Pretty underpinnings are just as important as what goes on top!

Daisy feels fresh as spring in her red, white and blue sailor outfit.

The sisters and Bertie all enjoy the garden in the summer sunshine.

Clusters of roses and ruffled lace trim Alice's charming party dress.

Bertie is unhappy because he wanted to go to the party too!

A quiet winter afternoon at home for the girls and their mischievous little dog.

Daisy and Bertie are going out to buy the ingredients for Alice to bake a cake.

The tired sisters are ready for bed – but Bertie must be tucked up first!

1 Cut the blouse front once, and the back and sleeve twice each: note the different sleeve lengths.

2 Join the front to the back at each shoulder. Press the seams open.

3 Turn under the edges of the centre back opening as indicated, and herringbone-stitch over the raw edges.

4 Bind the neck edge neatly.

5 Gather the top of each sleeve, as indicated. Then, right sides together, pin the sleeves into the armholes, matching side edges, notches, and centre top of sleeve to the shoulder seam. Draw up the gathers to fit and stitch carefully into position. Clip the curve carefully.

6 Join the side and sleeve seams.

7 Turn up a 1 cm (⅜ in) hem around the lower edge and herringbone.

8 **Alice:** Turn up the lower edge of each sleeve 1.5 cm (⅝ in). Turn the raw edge under and hem, forming a channel for the elastic.

9 **Alice:** Thread the elastic through, but *before drawing it up,* stitch lace very close to the lower edge so that it overlaps below and join the cut ends. Then draw up the elastic to fit, and knot securely.

10 **Alice:** Stitch lace *double* round the neck, the bottom edge of the lace level with the lower edge of the binding, to form a stand-up collar.

11 **Daisy:** Turn up the lower edge of each sleeve 2.5 cm (1 in). Turn the raw edge under and hem. Then stitch 1 cm (⅜ in) below, forming a channel for the elastic. Thread elastic through, draw up to fit, and knot securely.

12 Stitch snap fasteners to the centre back opening at neck, centre and waist, as O's on pattern.

13 Cut an 18 cm × 60 cm (7 in × 24 in) piece of fabric for the skirt as Fig 1. Cut Alice's waistband pattern twice in fabric, and her inner waistband once in Vilene. Cut Daisy's waistband pattern once in fabric.

14 Join the side edges of the skirt to form the centre back seam, leaving 6 cm (2½ in) open at the top for the centre back opening. Turn under the raw edges at each side of the opening and herringbone.

15 Mark the top edge equally into eight. Then gather 5 mm (¼ in) below the cut edge.

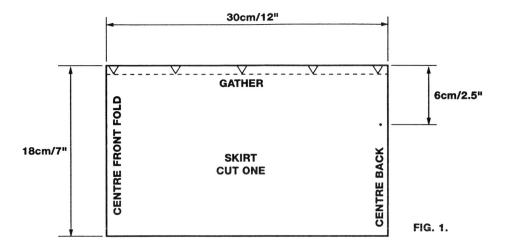

30cm/12"

GATHER

CENTRE FRONT FOLD

18cm/7"

6cm/2.5"

**SKIRT
CUT ONE**

CENTRE BACK

FIG. 1.

16 **Alice:** Tack the inner (Vilene) waistband to the wrong side of one waistband piece, the fabric overlapping equally all round. Then, right sides together and raw edges level, pin the top edge of the skirt to the lower edge of the interfaced waistband, matching the notches to the marked points, but have the waistband overlapping 5 mm (¼ in) at each end. Draw up the gathers to fit and stitch.

17 **Alice:** Right sides together, pin and stitch the second waistband to the first along the top and side edges. Clip the corners and curve closely, then turn to the right side. Turn the lower edge under and stitch neatly over the inside skirt gathers.

18 **Alice:** Glue narrow braid along the upper and lower edges of the waistband.

19 **Daisy:** Right sides together, pin the top edge of the skirt to the lower edge of the waistband, matching notches to marked points, but have the waistband overlapping 5 mm (¼ in) at each end. Draw up the gathers to fit and stitch.

 Right side inside, fold the waistband in half lengthways and stitch the cut ends. Clip the corners and turn to the right side, then turn the raw edge under and stitch neatly over the skirt gathers.

20 Turn up and herringbone a 2 cm (¾ in) hem around the lower edge of the skirt.

21 **Daisy:** Stitch a band of narrow ribbon round the skirt, 2 cm (¾ in) above the lower edge.

22 Sew a snap fastener to the waistband at the centre back.

23 For **Daisy's collar,** cut the back and front twice each (reversing the second front piece).

24 Right sides together, join the back pieces along the curved neck edge.

25 Open out the back and front pieces and, right sides together, join the front pieces to the back pieces at each shoulder, matching the notches, so that the centre top of each front is level with the ends of the neck seam. Clip and trim the seams carefully, especially the back neck.

26 Press the shoulder seams open before turning to the right side and re-folding each front down the centre, as the pattern. Press again, then tack the raw edges together.

27 Trim the raw edge level all round, then bind neatly.

28 Make a butterfly bow (Trims: Chapter 10) from the red ribbon, and stitch to the bottom corner of one front piece.

29 Stitch snap fasteners behind the bottom corner of each front piece, with the corresponding halves at the centre front of the waistband on the skirt.

Instructions for Alice and Daisy's **shoes** are in Chapter 9 (Accessories)

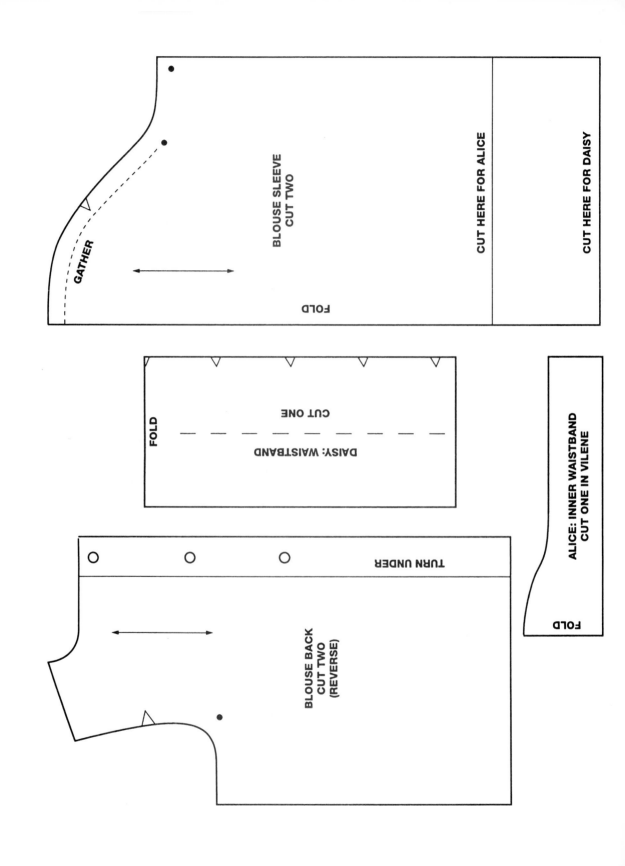

BLOUSE SLEEVE
CUT TWO

GATHER

FOLD

CUT HERE FOR ALICE

CUT HERE FOR DAISY

FOLD

DAISY: WAISTBAND

CUT ONE

ALICE: INNER WAISTBAND
CUT ONE IN VILENE

FOLD

TURN UNDER

BLOUSE BACK
CUT TWO
(REVERSE)

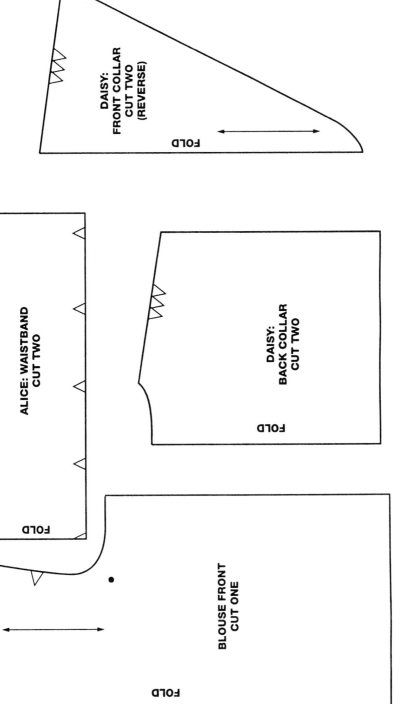

DAISY:
FRONT COLLAR
CUT TWO
(REVERSE)

FOLD

ALICE: WAISTBAND
CUT TWO

FOLD

DAISY:
BACK COLLAR
CUT TWO

FOLD

BLOUSE FRONT
CUT ONE

FOLD

Blouses and skirts are a perfect example of how to choose your fabric cleverly, in order to get the best out of it. Blouses generally call for a light-to-medium weight lawn or poplin, so that they tuck smoothly into the waistband of the skirt without looking bulky. Another very good reason for not using a thicker fabric is that on this small scale, it is much easier to set the sleeves in if you are working with a thin but firm fabric. Stitching the gathers in neatly, clipping the curves and sewing the underarm seams will all be much easier to do, and the finished effect will look far more like a genuine full-size garment in miniature.

All this would sound as if lawn was the ideal fabric to choose. This could well be so, but check first that white or pastel shades are not too see-through: you don't want their undies to show! On the other hand, if you are using a plain fabric, remember that a bit of lace will hide a multitude of patterned camisoles! You could have several slightly overlapping, horizontal rows of narrow lace creating a layered front panel; rows of very narrow lace forming vertical stripes down the front of the bodice, or a much deeper lace – 2–2.5 cm (¾–1 in) – gathered round the shoulders and curving down at the front, like Alice's party dress in Chapter 5.

Unlike blouses, skirts are straight and simple, without several converging layers of fabric to create problems of bulk. In addition, a full skirt needs to have enough body to stand out attractively and look feminine (if only to catch a glimpse of that pretty petticoat underneath). Daisy's nautical skirt, and Alice's deep rose version with its interesting curved waistband, both show just how ideal cotton sheeting is for this purpose. You can buy it in a good range of plain colours – Alice and Daisy particularly liked the deeper ones – or you can often find very attractive patterns on a small enough scale to be suitable such as tiny sprigs of flowers on a white background or white spots on a coloured ground. The one obvious drawback to cotton sheeting is that although you need only a short length, it's the width of a bed! Of course, this isn't a problem if you are making several dolls: even if the basic skirts were identical, you could make each one individual by adding different trimmings. However, if you are dressing only one doll, ask for the narrowest width (it's made to fit several kinds of bed, right up to king size), and choose a 'useful' colour that you will probably be able to use again in another guise. For instance, it's extremely good for small-scale upholstery if you are planning to treat your doll to some comfortable furniture like Alice and Daisy's.

The sisters trimmed their skirts in different ways with completely different kinds of decoration. Others might be two or three rows of narrow machine-embroidered ribbon or just one band of a wider striped or spotted ribbon; or a patterned ribbon, about 15 mm (⅝ in) wide, edged with plaited ribbon braid matched to three colours from the printed design; or how about a single ribbon rose at the centre of the shaped waistband, with a band of matching ribbon, edged with narrow black lace round the hem? These are just some of Alice and Daisy's imaginative suggestions!

Chapter 4

Alice's winter dress and pinafore/ Daisy's summer dress and bonnet

A practical dress pattern that can be interpreted in countless ways by your own choice of fabric and trimmings. Rag dolls don't feel the cold, so don't be tempted to choose a warm woollen fabric for Alice's winter dress as it will be difficult to work with and look too bulky when it is finished. The long sleeves and dark colour are sufficient to give an impression of warmth: a dress cotton with a dark background, or a medium-weight brushed cotton are good choices. On the other hand, Daisy's version couldn't look more summery, in cool blue with tiny puff sleeves and snowy white lace frills.

The narrow braid trimming the neck of Alice's dress is home-made, and picks up the two predominant colours of the floral design. The same type of braid on Daisy's version is just one colour, to match her dress but in a deeper shade.

Alice has a practical but pretty pinafore to protect her dress, whilst Daisy wears a face-flattering bonnet when she goes out in the sunshine.

For Alice's winter dress and pinafore you will need:

- ✄ 40 cm (½ yd) medium-weight cotton-type fabric, 75 cm (30 in) wide, for the dress
- ✄ A piece of medium-weight white cotton-type fabric, 15 cm × 25 cm (6 in × 10 in), for the pinafore
- ✄ 12 cm (5 in) lace, 1 cm (⅜ in) deep, for the collar
- ✄ 30 cm (12 in) and 15 cm (6 in) satin ribbon, 1.5 mm (¹⁄₁₆ in) wide, to make the collar braid (two-colour version)
- ✄ 70 cm (¾ yd) satin ribbon, 1.5 cm (⅝ in) wide, for the sash
- ✄ 50 cm (½ yd) white ribbon, 1 cm (⅜ in) wide, for the pinafore ties
- ✄ 60 cm (¾ yd) broderie anglaise, 2 cm deep, for the dress hem
- ✄ 1 m (1 yd) flat (unfrilled) broderie anglaise, 2.5 cm (1 in) deep, for the pinafore
- ✄ 12 cm (5 in) matching bias binding, to bind the neckline
- ✄ 20 cm (8 in) narrow round elastic, for the sleeves
- ✄ 3 snap fasteners
- ✄ Matching sewing threads
- ✄ Clear adhesive to fix the collar braid

For Daisy's summer dress and bonnet you will need:

- ✄ 30 cm (12 in) medium-weight cotton-type fabric, 90 cm (36 in) wide, for the dress and bonnet
- ✄ 70 cm (¾ yd) lace, 1 cm (⅜ in) deep, to trim the neck and sleeves
- ✄ 45 cm (½ yd) satin ribbon, 1.5 mm (¹⁄₁₆ in) wide, to make the collar braid (single-colour version)
- ✄ 60 cm (¾ yd) satin ribbon, 1 cm (⅜ in) wide, for the sash
- ✄ 40 cm (½ yd) of the same ribbon, for the bonnet ties
- ✄ 12 cm (5 in) matching bias binding, to bind the neckline
- ✄ 50 cm (20 in) narrow round elastic, for the sleeves and bonnet
- ✄ 3 snap fasteners
- ✄ Matching sewing threads
- ✄ Clear adhesive to fix the collar braid

1   **Winter version:** Cut a piece of fabric 18 cm × 60 cm (7 in × 24 in) for the skirt as Fig 1. Cut the dress front pattern once and the long sleeve and back twice each (reversing the second back piece).

   Summer version: Cut a piece of fabric 20cm × 60cm (8 in × 24 in) for the skirt as Fig 2, and another strip 15 cm × 50 cm (6 in × 20 in) for the bonnet front as Fig 3. Cut the dress front pattern once and the back, short sleeve and bonnet back twice each (reversing the second dress back).

2   Join the front to the back pieces at each shoulder. Press the seams open.

3   Gather the top of each sleeve as indicated. Then, right sides together, pin the sleeves into the armholes, matching side edges, notches, and centre top of sleeve to the shoulder seam. Draw up the gathers to fit and stitch into position. Clip the curves carefully.

4   Join the side and sleeve seams.

5   Turn up a 1.5 cm (⅝ in) hem around the lower edge of each sleeve. Turn under 5 mm (¼ in) and hem, forming a channel for the elastic.

6   Thread the elastic through and, for the **winter version** only, draw up to fit the wrists and knot securely.

   For the **summer version**, *before drawing up the elastic,* stitch lace very close to the lower edge so that it overlaps below. Then draw up the elastic to fit the top of the arm and knot securely.

7   Mark the top edge of the skirt equally into eight. Then gather 5 mm (¼ in) below the cut edge, beginning and ending 1 cm (⅜ in) from the side edges.

8   Right sides together and raw edges level, pin the lower edge of the bodice to the top edge of the skirt, matching the notches and side seams to the marked points. Draw up the gathers to fit, distributing them evenly between the pins, and stitch neatly together.

9   Join the side edges of the skirt, *making a 1 cm (⅜ in) wide seam,* and leaving open 6 cm (2½ in) at the top to form the centre back opening.

10   Turn under the centre back edges of the bodice as indicated, and 1 cm (⅜ in) along each side of the centre back opening of the skirt: herringbone-stitch over the raw edges.

11   Bind the neck edge neatly.

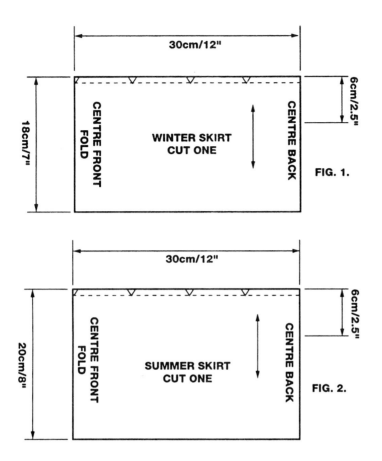

30cm/12"

6cm/2.5"

18cm/7"

CENTRE FRONT FOLD

CENTRE BACK

**WINTER SKIRT
CUT ONE**

FIG. 1.

30cm/12"

6cm/2.5"

20cm/8"

CENTRE FRONT FOLD

CENTRE BACK

**SUMMER SKIRT
CUT ONE**

FIG. 2.

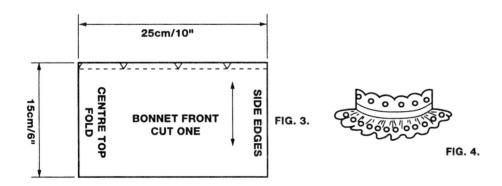

25cm/10"

15cm/6"

CENTRE TOP FOLD

SIDE EDGES

**BONNET FRONT
CUT ONE**

FIG. 3.

FIG. 4.

12 **Winter:** Stitch lace round the neck, the lower (straight) edge of the lace overlapping the top half of the binding so that the outer edge stands up above. Then make plaited braid (Trims: Chapter 10) and glue over the lower half of the binding.

Summer: As the winter version above, but before gluing the braid into position, gather 20 cm (8 in) more lace and pin it evenly directly below the lower edge of the binding, the outer edge of the lace in the opposite direction to the row above. Draw up the gathers to fit and stitch (Fig 4), then glue the braid into place.

13 Stitch snap fasteners at neck, centre and waist of bodice back opening.

14 **Winter:** Turn up a 1 cm (⅜ in) hem and herringbone over the raw edge. Then stitch broderie anglaise behind the hem so that it overlaps just below, as illustrated.

Summer: Turn up a 2 cm (¾ in) hem and herringbone over the raw edge.

15 Fit the dress on the doll and tie the sash round the waist, making a bow at the back. Trim the cut ends of the ribbon in an inverted V-shape.

16 **Pinafore:** Cut the apron pattern once, a strip 4 cm × 10 cm (1½ in × 4 in) for the waistband, and two straps, each 3 cm × 15 cm (1¼ in × 6 in).

17 Turn under and tack a narrow hem all round the sides and lower edge of the apron.

18 Gather a 45 cm (½ yd) length of broderie anglaise and pin the raw edge evenly all round behind the tacked edge. Draw up to fit, distributing the gathers evenly between the pins, and top-stitch very neatly into place.

19 Gather the top edge. Right sides together and raw edges level, pin one long edge of the waistband level with the waist edge of the apron, overlapping 5 mm (¼ in) at each end. Draw up the gathers to fit, distributing them evenly, and stitch.
   Turn under a 5 mm (¼ in) hem at each short end and tack. Fold the waistband in half lengthways, wrong side inside: turn the raw edge under and slip-stitch into place over the previous stitching line.

20 Cut the ribbon in half. Insert a cut end into each end of the waistband and stitch.

21 To make each strap, gather 23 cm (9 in) of broderie anglaise, then join to the strip of fabric as you joined the apron to the waistband, binding the fabric over the gathered edge of the broderie anglaise in the same way.

22 Overlap and join the straps in a V-shape, then stitch behind the centre of the waistband. Loop the back ends of the straps round the ties and stitch, allowing the ties to run smoothly through the loops.

23 **Bonnet:** Right sides together, join the two back pieces along the straight lower edge. Turn to the right side and tack together all round the curved edge.

24 Make a very narrow double hem along both short edges of the front strip. Mark one long edge equally into eight, then gather, beginning and ending 5 mm (¼ in) from the side edges.

25 Right sides together and cut edges level, pin the gathered edge round the bonnet back, matching the notches to the marked points. Draw up the gathers to fit, distributing them evenly between the pins, and stitch neatly together.

26 Gather across the lower edge of the bonnet back and draw up as tightly as possible.

27 Turn the front edge under 4 cm (1½ in): turn the raw edge under and hem. Then stitch the double fabric 1 cm (⅜ in) in front of the previous stitching line, to form a channel for the elastic.

28 Thread elastic through and draw up to fit round the face, as illustrated. Knot the ends and stitch them securely into place.

29 Cut ribbon in half and stitch over the ends of the elastic, for ties.

Instructions for their **shoes** and Daisy's **purse** are in Chapter 9 (Accessories).

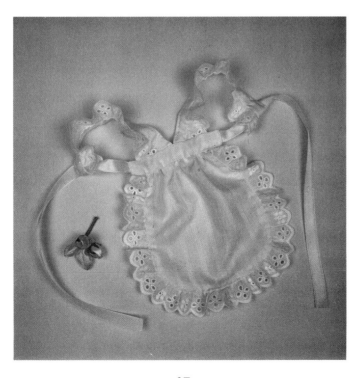

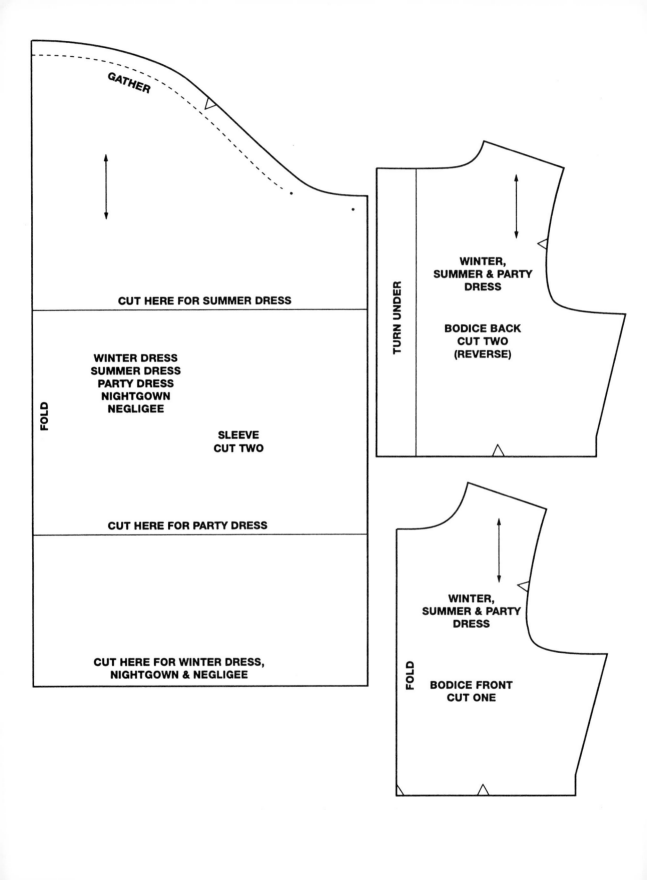

GATHER

CUT HERE FOR SUMMER DRESS

WINTER DRESS
SUMMER DRESS
PARTY DRESS
NIGHTGOWN
NEGLIGEE

FOLD

SLEEVE
CUT TWO

CUT HERE FOR PARTY DRESS

CUT HERE FOR WINTER DRESS,
NIGHTGOWN & NEGLIGEE

TURN UNDER

WINTER,
SUMMER & PARTY
DRESS

BODICE BACK
CUT TWO
(REVERSE)

WINTER,
SUMMER & PARTY
DRESS

FOLD

BODICE FRONT
CUT ONE

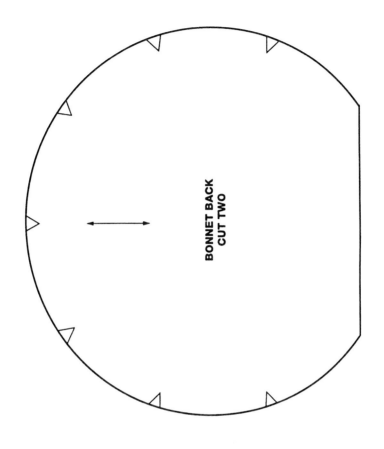

BONNET BACK
CUT TWO

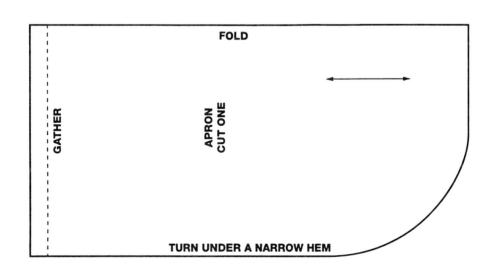

FOLD

GATHER

APRON
CUT ONE

TURN UNDER A NARROW HEM

Be warned: making dolls and, better still, dressing them, can be a bit addictive! But if you *are* aware of an overwhelming desire to go on creating little people in pretty dresses, you'll find it's a sure way to become extremely popular, and even discover friends you never knew you had. If this happens, then you might as well accept the fact that you have a fascinating new hobby and come to terms with it.

'Coming to terms with it' means keeping it at the back of your mind all the time and using your imagination. The most obvious time to do this is, of course, when you are in the dress fabric and haberdashery departments of your favourite store. If you see a fabric that has definite possibilities, *buy it*! Take advice from one who has learned from bitter experience that when you go back a week or two later, knowing just what you want, it's never there any more. As you can see from the amounts of fabric needed to make the garments in this book, you don't require very much to make a dress, and even less for a blouse or skirt. You'll have to buy only a few centimetres or a fraction of a yard and then it will be ready and waiting when you need it – whether it's next week or next year.

Time and time again I have congratulated myself of having had the foresight to buy a small piece of fabric that has proved exactly what I needed at a much later date. That's exactly what happened with both these dresses – I saw the fabric that eventually became Alice's winter dress in a small shop that was selling off all its stock in a closing-down sale, long before Alice was even a twinkle in my eye!

Sales are always a good time to keep your eyes open but you'll be lucky to find anything very exciting in the January sales. My favourite time is *afterwards*, when the winter sales have finally dragged to a halt. As soon as spring is in sight, the shelves suddenly blossom with spring and summer fabrics that might have been specially designed for Alice and Daisy and all their friends.

This is how I found Daisy's summer dress fabric. It was in pink or blue, amongst the bridal fabrics, and was intended for small bridesmaids. I bought both, and used the pink almost immediately to dress a baby doll for a nursery decoration. But the blue was so pretty that I kept it for three or four years waiting for a really special occasion to use it. So when Daisy needed a summer dress and bonnet, that seemed just the special moment I had been waiting for.

Trimmings, especially lace, are an even greater reason to go mad whenever you see something suitable. Whenever you see a pretty but inexpensive narrow cotton lace, grab it: you can be sure it will be used sooner or later. Buy several metres or yards, and hide it away in a secret place until you need it, because that's the one that everyone else wants too!

My favourite store has a very good selection of lace and broderie anglaise at various prices – some of them quite expensive – but they nearly always have lines that are comparatively cheap and just the thing to trim the kind of clothes that rag dolls wear.

Chapter 5

Alice's roses and lace party dress

❦

Alice is certain to be the most popular girl at the party in her delicate pink and white striped dress, lavishly trimmed with ruffled lace and clusters of satin roses in a deeper shade of pink. The finishing touch is her dainty lace hairband trimmed with more roses – as if she wasn't pretty enough already!

You may be surprised to find that this is the simple basic dress pattern, with a longer skirt and slightly shorter sleeves than the winter version. It's merely the addition of all those lace frills and the many-petalled roses that makes it so glamorous.

You will need:

- ✄ 40 cm (½ yd) medium-weight cotton-type fabric, at least 75 cm (30 in) wide
- ✄ 1.3 m (1½ yd) lace, 3.5–4 cm (1½ in) deep (double-edged, if possible), for the sleeves, skirt and hairband
- ✄ 50 cm (⅝ yd) lace, 1 cm (⅜ in) deep, for the collar and yoke
- ✄ 70 cm (¾ yd) satin ribbon, 1.5 cm (⅝ in) wide, for the sash
- ✄ 1.4 m (1⅝ yd) satin ribbon, 1 cm (⅜ in) wide, for the larger roses
- ✄ 3m (3⅜ yd) satin ribbon, 6 mm (¼ in) wide, for the smaller roses
- ✄ 12 cm (5 in) satin ribbon, 3 mm (⅛ in) wide, for the tiny rose
- ✄ 12 cm (5 in) bias binding to bind the neckline
- ✄ 20 cm (8 in) narrow round elastic for the sleeves
- ✄ 20 cm (8 in) *dark* elastic or hairgrips, to fix hairband (see Step 10)
- ✄ 3 snap fasteners
- ✄ Matching sewing threads

1   Cut a piece of fabric 22 cm (9 in) deep × 60 cm (24 in) wide for the party skirt as Fig 1. Using the basic **winter/summer dress** patterns, cut the bodice front once and the back twice (reversing the second piece). Cut the sleeve twice, to the length indicated on the pattern.

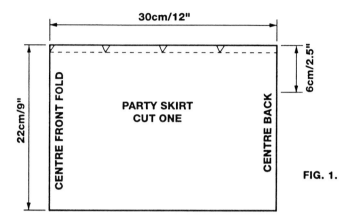

FIG. 1.

2   Follow the directions for the basic **dress**, Steps 2–11 inclusive, stitching the wide lace round the sleeves as instructed for the **summer** dress (Step 6).

3   Stitch narrow lace round the neck, the lower (straight) edge of the lace level with the lower edge of the binding, to form a tiny stand-up collar.

4   Gather the remainder of the narrow lace and pin it evenly round the bodice to form a yoke. The gathered edge of the lace should be level with the armholes at the outer ends of the shoulder seams, curving down to 2 cm (¾ in) at the centre front and back. Draw up the gathers to fit, distributing them evenly between the pins, and stitch neatly into position.

5   Turn up a 2 cm (¾ in) hem and herringbone-stitch over the raw edge.

6   Gather 90 cm (1 yd) of the wide lace about 5–10 mm (½–⅜ in) from the top edge (be guided by the lace design). Pin the lace evenly round the skirt, the lower (outer) edge 2 cm (¾ in) above the bottom of the hem. Draw up the gathers to fit, distributing them evenly between the pins, and stitch neatly into place.

7   Make six larger ribbon roses from 20 cm (8in) lengths of 1 cm (⅜ in) ribbon (Trims: Chapter 10). Make twelve smaller ones from 15 cm (6 in) lengths of the 6mm (¼ in) ribbon.
    Stitch a large rose at each side of the skirt, on top of the lace and about halfway down it. Stitch the other four large roses at equal distances between the side ones,

43

then stitch a pair of small roses at each side of the large ones, but slightly higher, as illustrated.

8 Make four more smaller roses and stitch two close together at the side of each sleeve, over the top edge of the lace.

9 Make a tiny rose from the 3 mm (⅛ in) ribbon, and stitch at the centre front of the neck.

10 Gather a 30 cm (12 in) length of lace down the centre for the hairband, as Fig 2, and draw it up to measure 15 cm (6 in). Join the outer corners of the cut edges at each end, as the arrows on the diagram.

 Make one more large rose and four smaller ones. Stitch the large rose in the centre, over the gathers, with two small ones at each side. Pin over the head, or fix with grips or elastic, distributing the gathers evenly.

FIG. 2.

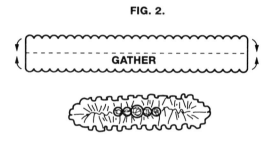

FIG. 3.

11 Fit the dress on the doll. Cut the ends of the widest ribbon in an inverted V-shape, then tie the sash round the waist, with a bow at the back.

Instructions for Alice's **shoes** are in Chapter 9 (Accessories).

Chapter 6

Daisy's hooded winter cape

Daisy is *never* satisfied, and when she saw this warm cape with its enchanting tartan-trimmed hood, she decided it would be even smarter if it made up into a complete outfit. So she thought hard and had a clever idea!

If *your* doll is just as difficult to please, buy 40 cm (½ yd) of 115 cm (45 in) wide tartan fabric and use **Daisy's skirt** and **blouse** patterns (Chapter 3), *omitting the collar,* to make a matching set to wear underneath the cape. You'll be able to cut the frill for the hood from the strip of fabric that remains when you have cut out the skirt. (Note: extra is allowed for matching tartan. If using a plain fabric, 35 cm (14 in) will be sufficient.)

You will need:

- ✄ 20 cm (¼ yd) felt (not too thin), 70 cm (27 in) wide
- ✄ A strip of medium-weight tartan fabric, 60 cm (24 in) wide × 8 cm (3 in) deep, for the frill
- ✄ 50 cm (½ yd) ribbon, 3 mm (⅛ in) wide, to make ties
- ✄ Snap fastener
- ✄ Matching sewing threads

1 Cut the cape and the hood patterns once each, in folded felt. Cut the frill in tartan fabric (if you are making a matching skirt, cut the hood frill at the same time).

2 Turn under and tack each end of the frill, then mark both long edges into sixteen equal sections, as indicated. Gather one long edge. Turn under a narrow hem along the other long edge and gather close to the fold (make sure your markings still show).

3 Mark the front edge of the hood into sixteen equal sections as indicated, on the right side. Right sides together and cut edges level, pin the *first* gathered edge of the frill along the front of the hood, matching the marked points. Draw up and stitch together, distributing the gathers evenly between the pins.

4 Mark the front edge of the hood into sixteen sections along the line of stitches on the wrong side. Then fold the frill along the centre, wrong side inside, and pin the gathered edge over the stitching line, matching the marked points. Draw up the gathers and slip-stitch the frill into place, distributing the gathers evenly as before.
    Oversew the short ends of the frill neatly, then tack and press the fold to give the frill a crisp edge.

5 Fold the hood in half, right side inside, and oversew the back seam. Open the seam out flat and then gather along it from the top corner to the notch. Draw up the gathers as tight as possible and finish off securely.

6 Gather the neck edge of the hood between the ends of the frill *(don't* gather the frill). Right sides together and raw edges level, pin the hood round the neck edge of the cape, matching the markings carefully and allowing the frill to overlap the front edges of the cape 1 cm (⅜ in).

7 Cut the ribbon in half and stitch a tie inside each front top corner of the cape. Stitch the top half of the snap fastener underneath one end of the frill, and the bottom on top of the other end, so that the frill is held together flat under the chin.

Instructions for **Daisy's muff** and **shoes** are in Chapter 9 (Accessories).

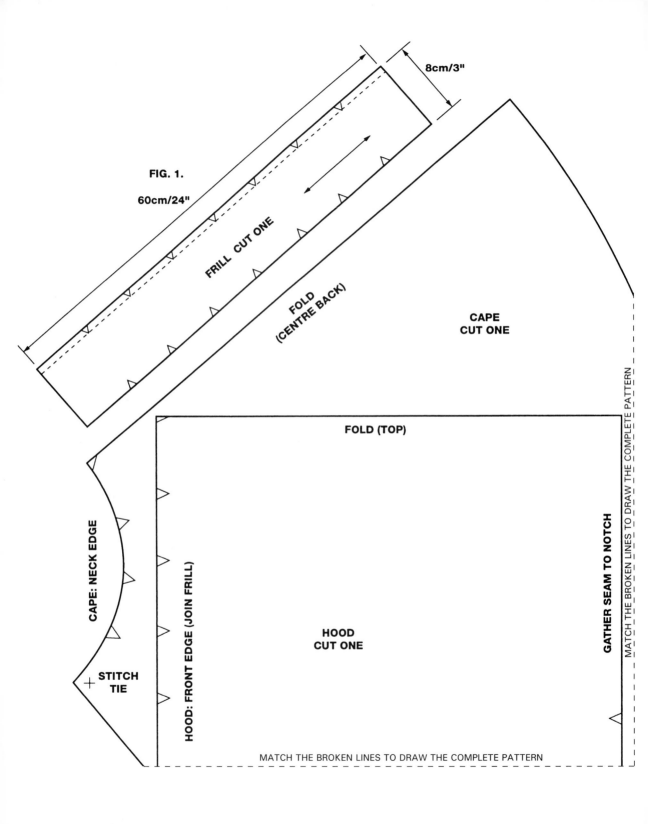

FIG. 1.

8cm/3"

60cm/24"

FRILL CUT ONE

FOLD (CENTRE BACK)

CAPE CUT ONE

FOLD (TOP)

CAPE: NECK EDGE

HOOD: FRONT EDGE (JOIN FRILL)

HOOD CUT ONE

STITCH TIE

GATHER SEAM TO NOTCH

MATCH THE BROKEN LINES TO DRAW THE COMPLETE PATTERN

MATCH THE BROKEN LINES TO DRAW THE COMPLETE PATTERN

MATCH THE BROKEN LINES TO DRAW THE COMPLETE PATTERN

MATCH THE BROKEN LINES TO DRAW THE COMPLETE PATTERN

HOOD: BACK

CAPE: FRONT EDGE

There is so little work in this cosy cape that it's made in next to no time, and if you replace the frill with a strip of fur fabric – it's finished in even less time than that!

It is no wonder that children enjoy using felt so much: not only does it come in a range of bright, attractive colours, but it's so easy to cut out, quick to sew and, as it can't fray, there are no raw edges to turn under, and no hems. And it answers all the problems of dolls who want to be smart but warm when they go out on a cold winter day!

I tend to repeat my warnings about avoiding thick, bulky, loosely woven woollen fabrics because I know how disappointing it can be to spend a lot of time and effort making something that ought to look wonderful when it is finished but doesn't, for a variety of reasons which cannot be rectified. Apart from the likelihood that fraying will make sewing a headache, thick fabrics mean doubly thick seams and turnings, with the result that the finished garment simply doesn't look as it should: like a miniature version of a full-size garment perfectly scaled down to fit a tiny person.

This is where felt steps in to save the day. The cape is just a very simple example of what it can do. Felt will make a smart tailored coat, beautifully fitted to flatter the figure: something you could never do with a thick fabric. Just as easily, it can be turned into a fashionable suit with a jaunty little braided jacket over a smoothly fitting skirt. It makes the most stunning hats too – all this with a minimal amount of sewing (you can find these in the follow-up book, *Alice & Daisy: special occasion outfits and furniture*, see the advertisement at the back of this book).

There are a few points to watch out for when buying your felt. First and foremost is quality, which is so important that it cannot be over-emphasised. Always look for felt that feels firm and smooth, and is an even thickness all over. Never buy one that feels thin, or has thin patches. At best your finished garment won't hold its shape well: at worst, the seams will pull away when it has been put on and taken off a few times. A slightly fluffy surface is another warning sign: as you work on it, the felt will produce even more fluff which will rub into tiny solid lumps, and spoil the finished garment. The effect is similar to the annoying 'pilling' that often happens to woollen jumpers.

It really is worth paying a little extra for a top quality felt: you won't regret it. If you need only a small amount – for shoes or other accessories – you can buy felt in squares. But for a garment, it is better to buy it by the metre or yard. You'll find you need less than you would to make a similar garment in a woven fabric, because you don't have to cut your pattern pieces according to the weave – you can place them in any direction, which makes felt very economical.

Well-chosen felt is the real secret of success. Once you have that, there are few rules to bear in mind. Oversew the seams neatly – preferably by hand – with tiny stitches in matching thread, 1.5–2 mm ($\frac{1}{16}$ in) deep is plenty. Then press the seams open carefully, ideally with a hot iron (use a damp cloth to be on the safe side). Remember these few points and you cannot go wrong.

Chapter 7

Daisy's Victorian nightgown

Choose a lightweight fabric with a dainty design for this romantic nightdress, with its long skirt falling from a high yoke. There are two ways to set in the sleeves – before you cut the armhole shaping (Step 2), see Step 8 so that you can decide which one is for you. The first method avoids having side seams, but the second is a little easier to do.

You will need:

- ✄ 30 cm (12 in) lightweight cotton-type fabric, 90 cm (36 in) wide
- ✄ 1.2 m (1¼ yd) lace, 1 cm (⅜ in) deep, for the neck, sleeves and hem
- ✄ 12 cm (5 in) satin ribbon, 3 mm (⅛ in) wide for the rose
- ✄ 12 cm (5 in) matching bias binding, for the neckline
- ✄ 20 cm (8 in) narrow round elastic for the sleeves
- ✄ 2 snap fasteners
- ✄ Matching sewing threads
- ✄ Clear adhesive to fix the rose (optional)

1 Use the **dress** pattern sleeve: cut this twice, side-by-side. Then use the remaining width of the fabric to cut a piece 30 cm (12 in) by at least 50 cm (20 in) wide (Fig 1), for the skirt. Finally, cut the front yoke pattern once and the back yoke twice (reversing the second piece).

2 Before cutting the armhole shaping, read Step 8. Then fold the skirt in half lengthways (centre front on Fig 2): mark the centre of the top edge with a pin, as indicated on the diagram. Place the armhole shaping pattern A or B (this is the shaded area on Fig 2) level with the top edge, the pin pointing down to the broken line. Cut out the curve.

   For method B *only,* cut down in the direction of the broken line to the lower edge, dividing the skirt into three – one front and two back pieces (see Fig 1).

3 Mark the top edge of the front skirt equally into four, then gather 5 mm (¼ in) below the cut edge, beginning and ending 5 mm (¼ in) from each armhole.

4 Right sides together and cut edges level, pin the lower edge of the yoke front to the top edge of the skirt, matching the notches to the marked points. Draw up the gathers to fit, distributing them evenly between the pins, and stitch neatly together.

5 Mark the top edges of each side of the skirt back into two, then gather as the front, 5 mm (¼ in) from the armhole edges, but 1 cm (⅜ in) from the centre back edge.

6 Join the skirt to the yoke back pieces as Step 4.

7 Join the yoke front to the back pieces at each shoulder. Press the seams open.

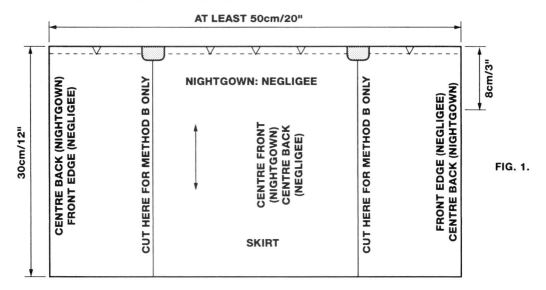

AT LEAST 50cm/20"

30cm/12"

8cm/3"

CENTRE BACK (NIGHTGOWN)
FRONT EDGE (NEGLIGEE)

CUT HERE FOR METHOD B ONLY

NIGHTGOWN: NEGLIGEE

CENTRE FRONT
(NIGHTGOWN)
CENTRE BACK
(NEGLIGEE)

SKIRT

CUT HERE FOR METHOD B ONLY

FRONT EDGE (NEGLIGEE)
CENTRE BACK (NIGHTGOWN)

FIG. 1.

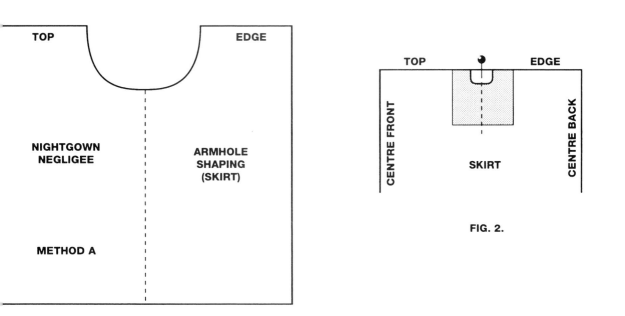

TOP   EDGE

NIGHTGOWN
NEGLIGEE

ARMHOLE
SHAPING
(SKIRT)

METHOD A

TOP   EDGE

CENTRE FRONT

SKIRT

CENTRE BACK

FIG. 2.

8 There are two ways to set in the sleeves. Decide which one you are going to follow before cutting the skirt.

Method A: Join the side seam of each sleeve. Gather round the top edge as indicated. Right sides together, pin the sleeve into the armhole, matching the notches

53

and the centre top of the sleeve to the shoulder seam. Make the sleeve seam central to the armhole curve in the skirt. Draw up the gathers to fit and stitch neatly together. Clip the curves carefully. If you are following this method, use the armhole shaping pattern A when you cut the skirt.

Method B: Gather round the top of each sleeve as indicated. Right sides together, pin the sleeves into the armholes, matching side edges, notches, and centre top of sleeve to the shoulder seam. Draw up the gathers to fit and stitch neatly into position. Clip the curves carefully, then join the sleeve seams and side seams of the skirt. If you are following this method, use the armhole shaping pattern B when you cut the skirt.

9   Turn up a 1.5 cm (⅝ in) hem around the lower edge of each sleeve, turn under 5 mm (¼ in) and hem, to form a channel for the elastic.

10   Thread the elastic through, but *before drawing it up* stitch lace very close to the lower edge so that it overlaps below. Then draw up the elastic to fit the wrists and knot securely.

11   Join the centre back edges of the skirt, *making a 1 cm (⅜ in) wide seam,* and leaving open 8 cm (3 in) at the top (below the yoke) to form the centre back opening.

12   Turn under the centre back edges of the yoke as indicated, and 1 cm (⅜ in) along each side of the centre back opening. Herringbone-stitch over the raw edges.

13   Bind the neck neatly.

14   Stitch lace round the neck over the binding, the straight edge of the lace level with the lower edge of the binding.

15   Join the cut ends of an 8 cm (3 in) length of lace and gather the straight edge, drawing it up to form a rosette with a 3 mm (⅛ in) diameter hole in the centre. Stitch to the centre front of the neck.

16   Make a ribbon rose (Trims: Chapter 10) and either glue or stitch in the centre of the rosette.

17   Stitch snap fasteners at the top and bottom of the yoke at centre back.

18   Fit the nightdress on the doll and turn up the hem. Turn the raw edge under and slip-stitch.

19   Stitch lace on the right side of the skirt, over the hem stitching line.

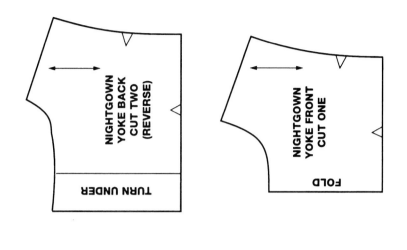

NIGHTGOWN
YOKE BACK
CUT TWO
(REVERSE)

TURN UNDER

NIGHTGOWN
YOKE FRONT
CUT ONE

FOLD

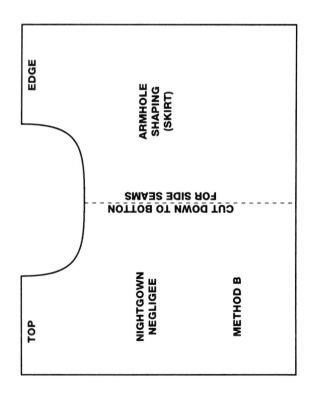

EDGE

ARMHOLE
SHAPING
(SKIRT)

CUT DOWN TO BOTTON
FOR SIDE SEAMS

TOP

NIGHTGOWN
NEGLIGEE

METHOD B

The nightdress pattern has so much potential. It easily becomes a negligée, but you could do a lot more if you think of it as being basically a loose garment falling straight from a small yoke. This style was very popular for children's clothes at the beginning of the twentieth century, so you could make a really true-to-period dress for your doll by simply making a shorter version of the nightgown. If you make an even shorter version – in plain white, without sleeves – you will have the kind of pinafore which little Edwardian girls wore over their dresses. The Sunday-best ones had a broderie anglaise frill round the edge of the yoke: a charming touch that would be worth copying!

Going to the other extreme, the negligée in Chapter 8 could be made in a plain dark fabric for a glamorous evening coat. Instead of gathering the sleeves in at the wrist, you might cut them a little shorter, then turn up a deep hem and leave them loose – perhaps adding a giant satin bow at the side of each sleeve and another at the neck. A soft lining satin would look wonderful for such a garment, but you would need to treat the cut edges with a fray-check product to seal them before you start sewing. If you are wary about using a fabric with a tendency to fray, you could make the coat in a jewel-coloured cotton poplin, and then add the luxury touch by trimming it lavishly with velvet tubing (by *Offray*) in either white or black.

Satin, and also taffeta, are such beautiful fabrics that it's a pity they are not easier to use for dolls' clothes. Their beauty lies in the way they reflect light so that they fall in gleaming folds of light and shade. Shot taffeta is especially effective, because the fabric is woven with either two different colours, or two shades of the same colour – one across the other. This means that in wear it catches the light from different angles, so that it changes from one shade to another with every movement.

If you are tempted to experiment with a slippery fabric like satin or taffeta, prevent the tendency to fray by sealing the cut edges before you start to sew, as before. Alternatively, you can also make things a lot easier for yourself by designing your garment cleverly, in order to emphasise the beauty of the fabric while avoiding the drawbacks.

For instance, the greatest problems lie in the bodice, where you have tiny curved seams, sleeve gathers and so on. So instead of making the whole dress in a problem fabric, you might make a plain top (black would be very sophisticated) from a 'safe' fabric like cotton poplin – or even felt – and then simply gather on a long strip of satin or taffeta for the skirt. This will give a spectacular effect without requiring any fiddly seams, because the satin or taffeta only has to be cut straight along the woven threads. Although sealing the cut edges would make things even tidier, it wouldn't be absolutely necessary if you used the fabric in this way.

When buying satin for this purpose, *don't* buy the best quality – you will find it is far too stiff and heavy for a doll. On such a small scale, you will get the best results from a good quality lining satin, which will drape and hang far more successfully yet gleam and shimmer just as effectively as one which costs ten times the price you paid!

Chapter 8

Alice's romantic negligée

The style of Alice's negligée is the same as Daisy's nightgown, and it has the same rose trim nestling in a flurry of lace, so the two would become a lovely set if made in the same fabric. Alice, however, has chosen a navy cotton spattered with tiny Valentine hearts to make her luxuriously full negligée even more romantic.

Like the nightdress, there are two ways to set in the sleeves. This part of the pattern is exactly the same as for the nightgown, so follow those instructions where directed. As before, read Step 8 for the nightgown to decide which sleeve method you wish to follow.

You will need:

- ✂ 30 cm (12 in) light or medium-weight cotton-type fabric, 90 cm (36 in) wide
- ✂ 12 cm (5 in) matching lace, 1 cm (⅜ in) deep, for the collar
- ✂ 8 cm (3 in) contrasting lace, 1 cm (⅜ in) deep for the rosette
- ✂ 12 cm (5 in) bias binding for the neckline
- ✂ 20 cm (8 in) narrow round elastic for the sleeves
- ✂ 2 snap fasteners
- ✂ Matching sewing threads
- ✂ Clear adhesive to fix the rose (optional)

1 Use the **dress** pattern sleeve: cut this twice, side-by-side. Then use the remaining width of the fabric to cut a piece 30 cm (12 in) deep by at least 50 cm (20 in) wide for the skirt as Fig 1 for the **nightgown**. Finally, cut the back yoke pattern once and the front yoke twice (reversing the second piece).

2 As Step 2 for Daisy's **nightgown,** following the same diagram and patterns.

3 Mark the top edge of the back skirt equally into four, then gather 5 mm (¼ in) below the cut edge, beginning and ending 5 mm (¼ in) from each armhole.

4 Right sides together and raw edges level, pin the lower edge of the yoke back to the top edge of the skirt, matching notches to the marked points. Draw up the gathers to fit, distributing them evenly between the pins, and stitch neatly together.

5 Mark the top edges of each side of the skirt front into two, then gather as the front, 5 mm (¼ in) from the armhole edges, but 1 cm (⅜ in) from centre front edges.

6 Join the skirt to the yoke front pieces as Step 4.

7 Join the yoke front pieces to the yoke back at each shoulder. Press the seams open.

8 As Step 4 for Daisy's **nightgown,** following the same diagram and patterns.

9   Turn up a 1.5 cm (⅝ in) hem around the lower edge of each sleeve, turn under 5 mm (¼ in) and hem, to form a channel for the elastic.

10 Thread the elastic through, draw up to fit the wrists and knot securely.

11 Fit the negligée on the doll and turn up the hem. Either turn the raw edge under and slip-stitch, or herringbone-stitch over the raw edge, according to the weight of the fabric.

12 Turn under the front edges 1 cm (⅜ in) and herringbone over the raw edge.

13 Bind the neck neatly.

14 Stitch matching lace round the neck over the binding, the straight edge of the lace level with the lower edge of the binding.

15 Join the cut ends of the contrasting lace and gather the straight edge, drawing it up to form a rosette with a 3 mm (⅛ in) diameter hole in the centre. Stitch to the (doll's) right front, at the base of the yoke, as illustrated.

16 Stitch snap fasteners at the neck and behind the rosette.

17 Make a ribbon rose (Trims: Chapter 10) and glue or stitch in the centre of the rosette.

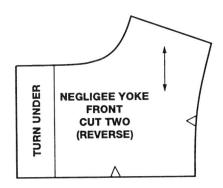

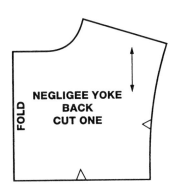

It's always the tiny finishing touches that add an extra dimension to an outfit. In this case it's a little lace rosette with a satin rose nestling in the centre: the same idea was also used on the nightgown. Under the long skirt of her negligée, Daisy is wearing matching navy blue slippers trimmed with a lace rosette with a white rose in the centre. Alice's slippers are pink, and have pink roses set in white lace. The finishing touches – a trim or a small accessory, like a muff or a purse – help to create a very special individual personality for your doll.

Just like the rest of us, every doll is different, and develops a character of its own. This happens automatically from the moment you begin to make your doll, but it becomes really noticeable after you have added the hair and features. By this time you will have a pretty good idea of your doll's natural personality, so from now on, you can emphasise the most obvious points. In Alice and Daisy's case it must be their femininity, their love of fashion, their affection for their dog, and – it has to be said – their vanity!

The following chapters contain some accessories that will give your dolls that extra finishing touch and show you how to make your own very individual trimmings. Do take advantage of them: your dolls will be so grateful! The ribbon roses in Chapter 10, for instance, can be used in a variety of ways to make a pretty item even prettier. Daisy's summer bonnet, in Chapter 4, would look so sweet with a cluster of tiny rosebuds at each side, or imagine how enchanting the bonnet would look in pale pink, with the rosebuds in a deeper shade of pink and matching ribbons. Daisy's little purse could go with it: the purse itself matched to the deeper pink, with the tiny roses that trim it in the paler shade of the bonnet.

The little butterfly bows in Chapter 10 are another example of a quick, easy and inexpensive trim that can work wonders on bonnets, purses, belts, shoes and hairstyles, as well as the garments themselves. As for the plaited braid, there is no end to the ways you can use this to lift a garment into the couture class. It's especially good on felt: the multicoloured version might be used to edge Daisy's cape (Chapter 6), for example. One length of ribbon could be matched to the green of the cape itself, and the other two to the purple and dark blue of the tartan. The result would be splendid and something you would never be able to achieve with a purchased braid.

Alice and Daisy's affair with fashion continues in their next book, where they are growing into still more clothes-conscious young ladies. They are even allowed to start putting their hair up for special occasions! As they become more and more involved in the social whirl, they need all kinds of outfits and their accessories become vitally important to create the total effect. Matching reticules and purses, parasols and umbrellas are necessary and, of course, no lady is ever seen out-of-doors without a hat. Needless to say, Alice and Daisy take all this very seriously – especially the hats, which range from a basic boater to wonderful confections of ribbons and roses.

Chapter 9

Alice and Daisy's accessories

Alice and Daisy's shoes

Make the shoes in black – either plain, as shown or as dancing pumps with long strings criss-crossed up the legs. Alternatively make coloured slippers with brown soles and perhaps a rose or butterfly bow trim at the front (Trims: Chapter 10).

You will need:

- ✄ 15 cm (6 in) square of felt
- ✄ Matching sewing thread

1 Cut the pattern for the upper four times and the sole twice.

2 For each shoe, join two uppers, oversewing at the front and back.

3 Pin the lower edge to the sole, matching the seams to the notches and oversew all round. Turn to the right side.

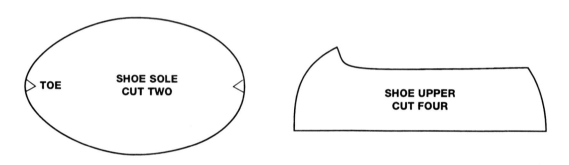

Daisy's white fur muff (Chapter 6)

Daisy snuggles her hands deep inside this cosy muff when she wears her hooded cape and it keeps them warm as toast! It's simplicity itself to make – just follow the diagrams.

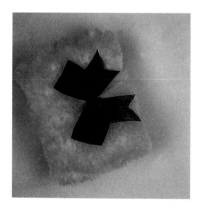

You will need:

- ✄ A 12 cm (5 in) square of fur fabric
- ✄ 15 cm (6 in) satin ribbon, 15 mm (5⁄8 in) wide, for the bow
- ✄ Matching sewing threads
- ✄ Clear adhesive (optional)

1 Cut the square of fur fabric in half as shown in Fig 1: *the arrows indicate the direction of the pile.*

2 Join A–A (oversew the cut edges), so that the pile runs in opposite directions (Fig 2). Then, right side inside, join B–B to C–C, forming a tube (Fig 3).

3 Turn the tube fur side out, folding flat so that the two joins are level in the centre. Then, right side inside (see direction of arrows on Fig 3 to determine right and wrong sides), join D–D to E–E (join the outside seam first, then the two inner edges over the top). Turn to the right side.

4 Make a butterfly bow with the satin ribbon (Trims: Chapter 10), and either stitch or glue it to the front of the muff.

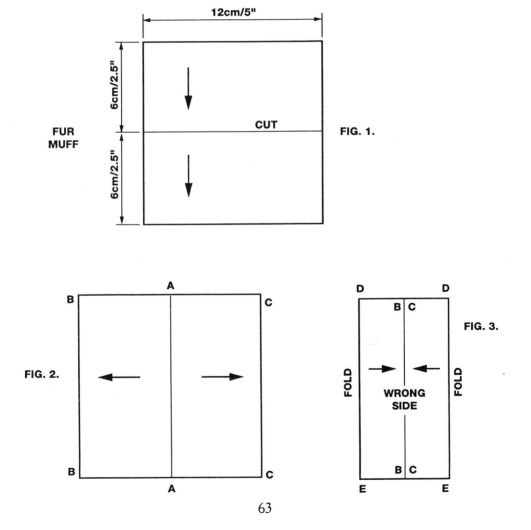

Daisy's rose-trimmed purse (summer dress)

Winter or summer, the girls like to carry their money and a spare hankie in a dainty little reticule, trimmed with beads and satin roses.

You will need:

- ✄ 6 cm × 8 cm (2½ in × 3 in) felt
- ✄ 10 cm (4 in) satin ribbon, 3 mm (⅛ in) wide, for EACH rose trim
- ✄ 12–15 cm (5–6 in) satin ribbon, 1.5 mm (¹⁄₁₆ in) wide, for a single handle OR 25–30 cm (10–12 in) crochet cotton or fine cord, for a double handle
- ✄ Small round bead for the clasp
- ✄ Small oval bead, and a tiny one to anchor it, for the bottom trim (optional)
- ✄ Matching sewing threads
- ✄ Clear adhesive

PURSE
CUT
TWO

1 Cut the purse twice in felt.

2 With the *wrong* sides together, either oversew or button-hole-stitch the two pieces neatly all round, leaving the top edge open.

3 Decide the length of handle required. Knot each end of the ribbon, or fold the crochet cotton or fine cord in half and then knot the ends. Insert the knots at each end of the top opening and stitch securely.

4 Stitch the round bead at the centre of the top opening so that it stands above.

5 If you wish, stitch an oval bead to the bottom point, anchoring it with a tiny one.

6 Make two ribbon roses (Trims: Chapter 10) and glue to one side, as illustrated.

Chapter 10

Make your own trims for pretty finishing touches

Finally, you can see how simple it is to make beautiful satin roses and dainty butterfly bows in any size, and also very narrow braid – all from ribbon! These make it possible for your dolls' clothes to have individual trimmings which not only perfectly complement their outfits, but are inexpensive too.

Ribbon roses

Ideally, use a single-face satin ribbon for roses, except for the 3 mm (⅛ in) ribbon, which comes only in double-face satin. This very narrow ribbon makes a charming miniature rose, but it is sensible to become familiar with the technique before attempting it, as it is a little more fiddly than the larger ones.

Choose a suitable colour: the *Offray* range of ribbons used on the projects in this book offers a wide choice of realistic shades that are as close as you can get to nature. On the other hand, unnatural colours can look just as attractive in certain situations. For example, dark brown or sable roses can look very elegant – so can navy, powder blue or grey!

You will need:

- ✂ Single-face (or double-face, see above) ribbon
- ✂ Matching sewing thread (*matching* thread is optional, as it won't show)

1 Cut off the required amount of ribbon: this will depend on the number of petals wanted, but the amounts shown below are a good average.

Width of ribbon	Length required
3 mm (⅛ in)	11 cm (4½ in)
6 mm (¼ in)	15 cm (6 in)
9 mm (⅜ in)	20 cm (8 in)
15 mm (⅝ in)	30–40 cm (12–16 in)

2 Fold the corner over, as shown by the broken line, bringing point A down to meet point B.

3 Bring point C over to meet points A and B.

4 Roll the ribbon around three or four times, with the folded corner inside, to form a tight tube, and make a few holding stitches through the base.

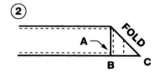

5 To make the petal, fold the ribbon down so that the edge is aligned with the tube. Then curve the ribbon around the tube to form a cone, keeping the top of the tube level with the diagonal fold.

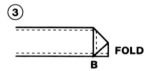

6 When the tube again lies parallel with the remaining ribbon, take a couple of stitches through the base to hold the petal you have just made.

7 Continue to make petals with the remainder of the ribbon, sewing each one to the base of the flower before starting the next.

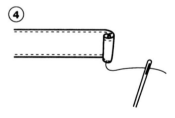

8 Shape the rose as you work by gradually making the petals a little more open. Finish with the cut end tucked neatly underneath the base of the completed rose.

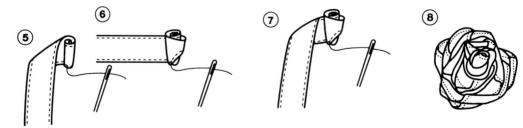

Butterfly bows

Use single-face or double-face satin ribbon. All the measurements for these bows are variable, so the length required will depend on the ribbon width, the effect you wish to create, and the length you want the streamers to be.

Experience and experimentation will determine your own personal preferences, but the examples shown here are a good average to work on for a standard shaped bow made from the narrower ribbon widths.

You will need:

- ✂ Single-face (or double-face) satin (or taffeta) ribbon (see below for amount)
- ✂ Matching thread

Width of ribbon	Length required
1.5 mm (1/16 in)	6 cm (2½ in)
3 mm (⅛ in)	8 cm (3¼ in)
6 mm (¼ in)	10 cm (4 in)
9 mm (⅜ in)	12.5 cm (5 in)
9 mm (⅜ in)	15 cm (6 in)

1   On the wrong (dull) side of the ribbon, mark point A at the centre, close to the lower edge as shown here. Mark points B and C equally either side of the centre, close to the top edge. Cut the ends in an inverted V-shape – or do this afterwards if you prefer – and don't do it at all for the narrowest ribbon.

2   Hold the ribbon with the wrong side facing you. Using matching thread, bring the needle through point A from the back. Then curve the left end round and bring the needle through point B: curve the right end round and bring the needle through point C. Draw up the thread so that B and C are on top of A.

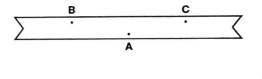

3 Take the needle up and through the centre top of the back part of the ribbon marked D on the diagram. Then take it down at the back and bring it through to the front again to emerge at point E on the diagram.

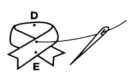

4 Take the thread up and over the top and wrap it tightly round the middle several times, drawing up and shaping the bow as you do so. Finish off neatly and securely at the back.

Plaited braid

Use 1.5 mm (1/16 in) wide satin ribbon. To estimate the amount you will need, measure the length of braid that you require, add a third of that length, and then multiply the result by three. As an example, for a 15 cm (6 in) length of braid, you will require:

15 cm + 5 cm (6 in + 2 in) = 20 cm (8 in)

20 × 3 = 60 cm (24 in)

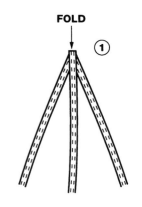

1 When using ribbon of one colour, fold the ribbon into three and cut *one* fold. Glue one end of the shorter piece inside the fold of the longer piece, as shown here, and pinch together. Glue in the same way if using two colours. If making a multicoloured braid, just glue all three cut ends together.

2 Push a pin through the glued end and secure it to a drawing board or something similar. Then begin to plait very evenly, making sure that the strands of ribbon are always flat – never fold them over. Keep the ribbon taut, and draw the plait very firmly between the fingertips every 2–3 cm (an inch or so) to make it smooth and even. Hold the ends together with a paperclip.

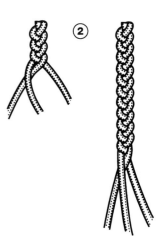

3 Glue the braid into place, spreading the glue on the braid just beyond the point where you intend to cut it, to ensure that it doesn't unravel. Press the cut ends down well, adding a little more glue if necessary.

Stockists and suppliers

Dress fabrics (including cream poplin), *Twilleys* stranded embroidery wools, knitting yarns, felt, lace and embroidered edgings and trimmings, sequins, *DMC* embroidery cottons, general sewing equipment, etc. are all obtainable from branches of the John Lewis Partnership. For further information or mail order: John Lewis plc, Oxford Street, London WlA lEX (Telephone: 0171 629 7711)

Offray ribbons: for your nearest stockist, write to: C. M. Offray & Son Ltd, Fir Tree Place, Church Road, Ashford, Middlesex TW15 2PH (Telephone: 01784 247281). Mail order from: Ribbon Designs, PO Box 382, Edgware, Middlesex HA8 7XQ (Telephone: 0181 958 4966).

UHU adhesives are available from all good stationers and craft shops.

The graph paper overleaf can be used to trace out patterns. Photocopy the relevant page (on page 70 each square = 1 cm and on page 71 each square = ½ in.) a number of times and then tape the photocopies together to make one large sheet. Fix your tracing paper on the top to rule out accurate patterns from the diagrams.

Use this grid if you are working with metric measurements: each square = 1 cm.

this grid if you are working with metric measurements: each square = ½ in.

Alice & Daisy

Special occasion outfits and furniture

Valerie Janitch

(ISBN 1 85486 184 0)

In this follow-up book, designer Valerie Janitch provides the solution to the perennial problem of what a rag doll with a busy social life should wear!

This book includes patterns and detailed directions for a whole variety of special occasion fashions. Daisy is especially thrilled with her demurely pretty bridesmaid's outfit – and delighted with the latest thing in bathing costumes, complete with frilly cap, for her seaside holiday. While Alice has a romantic ballgown to keep her waltzing until dawn, and a particularly elegant coat plus matching hat and accessories for winter trips to town.

Alice and Daisy seldom go anywhere without their little dog, Bertie, who is nearly as fashion conscious as they are! This book shows you how to make him as well as full instructions for furnishing Alice and Daisy's home. Everything is easily made from cardboard covered with fabric or paper. No hammers, saws, nails or screws are needed – just glue!

This title should be available from good bookshops. In the event of difficulty please contact the Books Division, Nexus Special Interests Ltd., Nexus House, Azalea Drive, Swanley, Kent BR8 8HU Tel: 01322 660070.